From Bad Faith to Good News

ALISTAIR KEE

From Bad Faith to Good News

Reflections on
Good Friday and Easter

SCM PRESS
London

TRINITY PRESS INTERNATIONAL
Philadelphia

First published 1991

SCM Press
26–30 Tottenham Road
London N1 4BZ

Trinity Press International
3725 Chestnut Street
Philadelphia Pa. 19104

British Library Cataloguing in Publication Data

Kee, Alistair
From bad faith to good news.
1. Christian Church. Easter
I. Title
263.93

ISNB 0–334–02489–7

Library of Congress Cataloging-in-Publication Data

Kee, Alistair. 1937–
From bad faith to good news : reflections on Good Friday and Easter / Alistair Kee.
p. cm.
Includes bibliographical references.
ISBN–0–334–02489–7
1. Jesus Christ—Passion—Sermons. 2. Jesus Christ—Resurrection—Sermons. 3. Sermons, English. I. Title.
BT431.K44 1991
232.96—dc20 90–22831

Phototypeset by Input Typesetting Ltd, London
and printed in Great Britain by
Clays Ltd, St Ives plc

CONTENTS

PROLOGUE

When I mentioned to friends and colleagues that I had agreed to conduct a three-hour Good Friday Meditation they were surprised. I was amazed. In March 1989, during my first year of teaching at Edinburgh University, I received an invitation from Canon Neville Chamberlain, Rector of St John the Evangelist, Princes Street, to conduct the Good Friday Meditation. I should make it clear that the invitation was for a year thence, March 1990. This Neville Chamberlain is a man of foresight. While it was not something for which I should have volunteered, when I got down to the actual preparation of the material I was glad that I had agreed, and grateful for the invitation.

Although I had taught a course on the Gospels throughout most of my academic career this was a very different experience. For one thing I had to go back to the texts themselves, to read them as narratives. Very often critical commentaries deal with issues which are never more than peripheral prolegomena. They clear the ground but they do not build. More importantly, preparing the meditations enabled me to examine as a practical matter an issue which had engaged me at an academic level as a graduate student: the relationship between the historical Jesus and the Christ of faith. The more I pored over the texts the more I was convinced that the specifically Christian character of faith emerges in the experience of Jesus in Gethsemane and on the cross.

By that I certainly do not mean that kind of neurotic dwelling on the actual suffering of Jesus, psychologically and physically, which passes for profound spirituality. Many of the assumptions of traditional theology and the piety associated with it disguise from us the real significance of those last events in the life of Jesus. What is clear is that nothing was clear: but he continued with the path set before him. This is the nature of faith, as of life. Luke tells us at the beginning of the story that Jesus 'increased in wisdom' throughout his life. But *prokoptein*, to make progress, was a verb used of an army hacking its way with excruciating difficulty through the impediments in its path. And Barth once observed that it was a term used when a blacksmith increased or extended a piece of metal by pounding it again and again with hammers. How Jesus increased in wisdom and continued to do so even till those last and terrible hammers of Golgotha deserves to be studied in its own terms. It needs no aesthetic addition for dramatic effect. Nor effete pondering over the pain. Without such distractions it goes directly to the most profound levels of experience.

I am more accustomed to speaking in a lecture room than from a pulpit. More available to be interrupted for clarification. Standing as it were within spitting distance of my audience. When I first began my career as a lecturer we used to illustrate our topics with allusions to a rich variety of literary sources – or so it seems to me with the embellishment that comes with the passing years. Now, alas, we are more likely to say to students, Did you see that programme on TV last night? When I was attempting to identify the perspective of these meditations, the theme which would hold them together, it was therefore not surprising that a phrase came to me not from classical prose but from a TV quiz programme. In it contestants are presented with a collage of images which suggest a well known phrase. If they begin to theorize about it they are lost. The quiz master reminds them, 'The clue is in the picture.' It is *in* the picture itself. In preparing these meditations I became increasingly convinced that the mystery is *in* the events. I therefore reassurred the congregation that they must travel light: little theology and no metaphysical theories. The mystery is *in* the events, not in a theological interpretation of them. They are not metaphors or symbols of a higher metaphysical order. The mystery is *in* the events, in our history, in our human lives. This is what incarnation means. The mystery and the revelation unfold within the human experience of Jesus and his followers. If the mystery and revelation could have been manifest in some other way then Jesus need not have suffered and died. His death would not be real.

The mystery is *in* the events. That seems straightforward enough, and yet on closer inspection it is the reverse of what so often happens. More often the meaning and significance of the events are replaced by theories about them, as if we already knew what they revealed without attending to them. As Husserl put it in developing his phenomenological method, 'To the things themselves.' If we could set aside for the time being the assumptions we make, which protect, insulate and isolate us from the reality of the events, then we might encounter the true mystery of the cross.

We have good reason to think that we stand at a higher point of history than those who came before us. We shake our heads at the thought that people ever believed the world to be flat. We have seen photographs of Earth taken from its moon. (They really did go there, didn't they?) We find incredible the first heresy in the Christian church, Docetism. The name comes from the Greek word *dokein*, to seem. The Docetists are often referred to as if they were an organized group. In the language of sectarian politics we should probably see them as a tendency. Within the Christian church some people fell into this way of looking at things. They believed that Jesus only seemed to be a man, only seemed to suffer, only seemed to die. It sounds incredible. Yet the first heresy is the most persistent. It has been constantly present in the history of the church. It has infiltrated orthodox belief, and it represents the majority view among Christians in the modern world. It stands for the rejection of the view that the mystery is *in* the events.

Docetism, condemned as the first heresy, is alive and well whenever it is thought that Jesus had to be born in some way different from human beings, to protect him from being human. It is present whenever it is thought that Jesus did not need to live by faith because he already knew everything that was going to happen. Ancient Docetism is present today when Christians think that Jesus did not go down into death as other human beings do, that he knew in advance that he would rise again on the third day. Through this false theology, this metaphysical theory, Christians are distracted from the events themselves, from the mystery which is revealed *in* them. In this way the life and death of Jesus are abstracted from our history and become events in a higher history quite different from ours. We may smile at the ancient heresy, but like Satan at the temptations, it has only withdrawn strategically, to return at an opportune time. At Christmas we join with the shepherds in saying 'Let us go even to Bethlehem, and see this thing that has happened . . . ' On this Good Friday let us go even to Gethsemane and Golgotha, because the mystery which is *in* these events is far more mysterious than any theory ever devised about it by men in ancient times or in the modern world.

The preparation for the meditation was therefore of great value to me personally, and I hope it was of some value for those who joined together on Good Friday. But I am more experienced as a writer and not surprisingly I found it easier to prepare the material as if I were writing the chapters of a book. The six chapters of Part One therefore arose from the six meditations presented in the Church of St John the Evangelist, Princes Street, Edinburgh on Friday 13 March 1990. They end with Jesus betrayed, denied and forsaken by his disciples and friends – at the least the male disciples. They end with the Cry of Dereliction: Jesus forsaken by God. They end with the women sitting across from the tomb, at the end of the longest and blackest day of their lives. The end of the story comes at the end of the day as night falls and God's sabbath begins. I felt it important to finish the Good Friday meditation on that note. The jury was out, so to speak. What would be the verdict on Jesus when life started again after the sabbath? Unless we see what is at stake at that point we shall not understand the new faith which was soon to appear.

But it would be a strange and eccentric point at which to end a Christian work, and therefore I have extended the book into Part Three. These are reflections on Easter and the nature of Christian faith and experience. But the two belong together. Until we watch with Jesus in Gethsemane and follow him in that Descent into Hell, we shall not understand the nature of his victory, and its significance for us.

Glasgow
Whitsun 1990

PART ONE

Bad Faith

1

The Prisoner of Conscience

(*a*) *From poll tax to cross*

We are gathered here today to recall the life and death of Jesus of Nazareth. And what have these events to do with us? They come to us as from a different world, remote in time and place. How can events from such a primitive and peripheral society have anything to do with us in our sophisticated and advanced culture? What can such stories tell us about our lives, let alone our salvation? That remains to be seen, but let us not assume too quickly that the events of the life and death of Jesus are alien to our world or our experience.

The story begins with a couple who were travelling. Now that area is awash with tourists, but it was not by choice that they were on the road, especially since the young woman was in the last days of her pregnancy. In 1982 I lived in America, in the southern states, and every day cars flooded down Interstate 95 towards Florida. But not all of their occupants were making the trip for pleasure. Reaganomics were beginning to have their effect, and many of these unwilling travellers had lost their homes and were now forced to live in their cars. Not all families who travel do so by choice, even in tourist areas. Our story begins not in a car but in a stable, which contrary to romantic Christmas cards is more likely to have been infested with fleas and rats. And all this because of the poll tax. The baby was born in a stable because an autocratic governor, who did not even live in that country, decided to impose a poll tax. I mention this fact to remind us that the world in which Jesus lived, remote in time and place, was in fundamental respects very much like ours. Indeed if his world had not been like ours, marked by homelessness, illegitimacy, injustice, jealousy and pettiness, torture and arbitrary execution, then we need not meet here after all.

Not that scholars would necessarily accept all the material about the life of Jesus as being historically accurate. No sacred book has been subjected to so much unbridled criticism as the Bible. It is assumed that the events in the life of Jesus are being presented to suit the purposes of the early church. And if that were so, what a poor job they made of it. If you were trying to promote your hero and gain support for his cause how would you begin? Would you recommend him to new converts by saying that he came from a very good family, or that he was conceived in dubious circumstances? Would you say he was born in a manor house, or at least in a private nursing home? Or would you say that he was born in a stable? But of course all of these points are as nothing compared with how it was all to end. It is said that the Gospels were written backwards. The writers knew from the outset how the story was to end, and they wrote towards it. One third of Mark's Gospel deals with the last few days of the life of Jesus. And what did the writers have to fear about putting their readers off by reference to the conception and birth compared with the scandalous outcome, that Jesus had been executed? Worse than that, crucified by the imperial governor. Who would begin with such an account if it were not inescapable, if it were not in fact the very truth of the matter? The life that began in circumstances imposed by the Romans ended in the same way. Where was the freedom and hope in that?

(*b*) *Arrest*

We begin the story as events move to their dramatic and tragic climax. It is ironic that Christianity, for so long associated in Europe with law and order, begins with the arrest of its founder by the authorities. Jesus was arrested. No, he was not assisting the police with their enquiries. The authorities knew the man they wanted. It was not a case of mistaken identity. Being arrested means different things in different circumstances. When we hear that someone has been arrested for stealing a hand bag we know that this is a petty criminal who deserves to go to prison. When we hear that someone has been arrested for insider dealing in the city worth £1M we know that this is the result of a thrusting entrepreneur going a bit too far. When a political figure in the USA is caught with his hand in the till people simply shake their heads as if corruption in public life is as American as apple pie.

But there is another context of arrest, and if anything it is more common in the last thirty years. It is exemplified in the Civil Rights movement in America in the 1960s. Its motive is public good, not private greed. It arises not from disregard of the law, but from commitment to a higher law; that law by which laws are judged. We see it in those inspiring figures, many of them black, who marched at the front of demonstrations; men and women, bold and brave. And if anything we see it more clearly in those who came behind them, not at all bold or brave, but alarmed and apprehensive, and who for that very reason exhibited even greater courage. When arrested they became prisoners of conscience.

Jesus was arrested. Surely not. There must be a mistake. Far from it. Jesus was arrested, and knew weeks and months before the event that it would certainly come to this. To think that it was a mistake or in some way avoidable is to misunderstand the significance of Jesus and to fail to grasp what was at stake. In the Gospels Jesus predicted his arrest on three occasions. It may have come as a complete surprise to his followers, but not to Jesus. 'From that time Jesus began to show his disciples that he must go to Jerusalem and suffer many things from the elders and chief priests and scribes and be killed . . . ' (Matt 16.21). And of course this final confrontation would only take place if Jesus went to Jerusalem. If it did not happen in the capital it would not really have happened. (Does anything change?) ' . . . it cannot be that a prophet should perish away from Jerusalem' (Luke 13.33). Some scholars have questioned whether Jesus predicted his death in Jerusalem, but with respect it would not take the gift of prophecy to see what was coming. According to Mark the ministry of Jesus had scarcely begun before he had alienated the most powerful groups in society, both religious and political. 'The Pharisees went out, and immediately held counsel with the Herodians against him, how to destroy him' (Mark 3.6). If these are simply names to readers today then the significance of the alliance will escape us. It would be like a meeting in Northern Ireland between Ian Paisley and Gerry Adams. If one group did not get to him the other would. And so the prediction is more like a statement of fact than an inspired vision.

> Behold we are going up to Jerusalem; and the Son of man will be delivered to the chief priests and scribes, and they will

> condemn him to death, and deliver him to the Gentiles to be mocked and scourged and crucified . . . (Matt 20.18–19).

It may be that Jesus envisaged that he would be killed by the Jews rather than the Romans. 'O Jerusalem, Jerusalem, killing the prophets and stoning those sent to you!' (Luke 13.34). But of the inevitable confrontation he was in no doubt. His fate, it would seem, was sealed.

But this was not in fact the case. The strong impression we get from the Gospels is that Jesus was in control of events, even the events leading to his arrest and execution. The arrest would take place only when he went up to Jerusalem. He chose the time: the Passover, that central feast of the Jewish liturgical year when they recalled their deliverance from an imperial power and their vocation to be a people obedient to God. Jesus chose his time, but he also chose the place of his arrest. We gather from the Gospels that he had a considerable popular support in Jerusalem. His criticism of the religious establishment endeared him to the people.

> When the chief priests and the Pharisees heard his parables, they perceived that he was speaking about them. But when they tried to arrest him, they feared the multitudes, because they held him to be a prophet (Matt 21.45–6).

If Jesus had sought to avoid arrest then he would not have gone to Jerusalem, or having gone there would have slipped away. Alternatively he could have remained in the city, safe among his popular support. Instead he left this security for the near-by Mount of Olives, and the Garden of Gethsemane. To this scene we shall return later, but here we have the paradox that the wanted man has arranged the time and place of his arrest: the one who is sought has made sure he can be found.

All this we can understand very well. We know of prisoners of conscience who will not flee, because this would somehow give the victory to those who are the real wrong-doers. The real wrong-doers will not be confronted and exposed until the prisoner of conscience is arrested. And so the guards proudly brought Jesus before the Sanhedrin, the Jewish Supreme Court, or at least a quorum. They the judges, he the accused. If only they had known.

(*c*) *The process*

Television has divided history. We now know of things we have never experienced. Or rather through television in a real sense we have experienced them. Thus we know about the consistency of the surface of the moon and forms of life at the bottom of the ocean. And of course we know about courtrooms and trials. Even those who have never had cause to be in a court of law can both picture the scene, and know about due process. But in the case of the trial of Jesus, the most famous trial in history, this knowledge is of little help. As scholars point out, it is unlikely that the immediate followers of Jesus would have access to the proceedings. The details of the trial come from no transcript. Indeed it would seem to reflect what the early church assumed to have taken place. Viewed more closely, it is a very confusing account. Or rather there is a contrast between the integrity of the prisoner of conscience and the dishonesty of those who conspired against him. There is the contrast between the stormy scenes of false witness, convoluted argument, rage and fear – a contrast between that and the one who stands as a calm centre, a silent witness to the truth.

Surprisingly it is not even clear what the charge was against Jesus. Was he the Messiah, the Christ? But it was not a crime to claim to be Messiah. At least not a crime under Jewish law. It was of course a crime under Roman law, and it would seem from the superscription on the cross that this was the charge on which he was condemned by Pilate. This was also the central claim of the early church, as reflected in the first sermon by Peter in Acts: 'Let all the house of Israel therefore know assuredly that God has made him both Lord and Christ, this Jesus whom you crucified' (Acts 2.36). It would therefore seem reasonable to assume that this was the basis of the trial before the Sanhedrin. The Jews rejected Jesus as the Christ. But as we have observed, it was not a crime to claim to be the Messiah and Jesus could not have been condemned simply on this basis. Indeed it is unlikely that Jesus even claimed that title for himself during his lifetime. The issue was at once more general than that, and more fundamental.

If Jesus anticipated death at the hands of his own people, by stoning, then the issue must have been that of authority. As early as the Sermon on the Mount this was clear. ' . . . the crowds were astonished at his teaching, for he taught them as one who had authority, and not as the scribes' (Matt 7.28–9). The authority also extended to his power of evil spirits. 'With authority he commands even the unclean spirits, and they obey him' (Mark 1.27). It is on the question of authority that he was drawn into conflict with the chief priests – the authorities.

> One day, as he was teaching the people in the temple and preaching the gospel, the chief priests and the scribes with the elders came up and said to him, 'Tell us by what authority you do these things, or who it is that gave this authority?' He answered them, 'I will also ask you a question; now tell me, Was the baptism of John from heaven or from men?' And they discussed it with one another, saying, 'If we say, "From heaven", he will say, "Why did you not believe him?" But if we say, "From men", all the people will stone us; for they are convinced that John was a prophet.' So they answered that they did not know whence it was. And Jesus said to them, 'Neither will I tell you by what authority I do these things' (Luke 20.1–8).

Jerusalem killed prophets and stoned those sent to it. The authorities would not accept any other authority. For the prophet to claim the direct authority of God was therefore in their eyes blasphemy. And this was the charge on which Jesus was condemned. It is at once more general than claiming to be the Christ, but at the same time more fundamental. If Jesus taught the true knowledge of God, indeed if he embodied the truth about God, then this was the ultimate confrontation with the authorities, more profound than title of Messiah.

It is of interest therefore that before the trial began Luke tells us that his captors began to abuse Jesus, blindfolding him, striking him and calling out 'Prophesy! Who is it that struck you?' (Luke 22.64). At the Jewish trial he was mocked as a prophet. Later at the Roman trial he would be mocked as a king.

We have already noted that the trial was very confusing. The defendant was completely in control. It was the prosecution who were in disarray. Did he threaten to pull down the temple? Or did he prophesy that it would happen? To condemn an innocent man it is necessary to employ false witnesses. But Mark tells us 'Yet not even so did their testimony agree' (Mark 14.59). Clearly some one in the Prosecution Service had slipped up. When I worked in Rhodesia some twenty-five years ago, before it was Zimbabwe, I appeared in court as a defence witness for one of my students who had been arrested on a demonstration. Against me appeared some eighteen police officers. They all repeated the same version of the events, verbatim. It was false witness, and one of the marks of false witnesses is that they agree in great detail. But in the Gospel account of the trial the prosecution could not produce witnesses who were false enough. The outcome was therefore to re-enforce the picture of the prisoner of conscience who was completely in control. They could not make a case against him. They could not convict him even by false witnesses. In the end the high priest had to appeal to Jesus to help them. He had to provide them with the evidence on which they could convict him. In other words, even at this late stage Jesus could have withdrawn from the contest. He would have saved his life, but at the cost of his soul. It was by his permission that they were able to act. The prisoner was the only free man in court. His silence was testimony to God's truth. Their words exposed not his blasphemy but their own: by their condemnation of him his judges in turn were judged.

(*d*) *The free man*

This is the paradox of the prisoner of conscience, the man who is freer than his captors, who may give his life to keep his soul. Nor is this metaphysical theology of a particularly obscure form. We understand these things very well in the modern world, if we have eyes to see.

As I was preparing these meditations we witnessed a remarkable example of this in the case of Nelson Mandela. At the beginning of February 1990 speculation was rife: would he be released tomorrow or next week? But this was no ordinary prisoner. President P.W. Botha wished to release him, but he would not leave prison, at least not on the terms offered. F.W. de Klerk had to negotiate with him in order to get him to accept freedom. Even the world media could see the reversal: the prisoner was the free man, who had power over his captors. The man in prison was truly free because he had dedicated his life to a moral cause. It was that cause which was to judge the judges. It could not be defeated, nor could he. In 1964 at the end of the Rivonia trial Nelson Mandela concluded the speech in his own defence with these words:

> During my lifetime I have dedicated myself to this struggle of

> the African people. I have fought against white domination, and I have fought against black domination. I have cherished the ideal of a democratic and free society in which all persons live together in harmony and with equal opportunities. It is an ideal which I hope to live for and to achieve. But if needs be, it is an ideal for which I am prepared to die.[1]

Mandela was convicted on the 11 June 1964. On the 11 February, 1990, on his release from prison he ended his first speech with these same words. We must not forget or seek to romanticize for a moment the real suffering and privations of these long years. But with his release the judges were judged. It was he who had been on the side of justice and truth: they had been the instruments of injustice and falsehood.

Jesus wrote nothing of his teaching or experience, but in modern times there has arisen a considerable body of literature which could be described as Prison Writings. These are remarkable testimonies by prisoners of conscience. They are not of course the normal letters from convicted criminals, still protesting their innocence, still embittered about those fellow felons who let them down. Instead we have what could not be predicted, a spirituality which arises from imprisonment.

Examples of this are to be found in the works of another prisoner of conscience, the Russian writer Alexander Solzhenitsyn. In February 1956 the Military Collegium of the Supreme Court of the USSR met and revoked his conviction. The judges were judged and the prisoner vindicated as the man of truth. In 1945 this twice decorated captain of the artillery had been sentenced to eight years of hard labour in prison camp for some critical remarks he had made about the government. Two years after his release he began work on the book which was later to be published as *The Gulag Archipelago*. One of the most unexpected and disturbing themes which runs through the book is its spirituality, for want of a better name. Many prisoners in the labour camps died of the cruel conditions and the harshness of the regime. But beyond that Solzhenitsyn tells us that they perished within themselves. Having lost everything, they died. A few, like Solzhenitsyn, had a very different experience. He could compare the prisoner and the monk: both were spared the distractions of property, the continual dissipation of life. He speaks of

> . . . that glimmering light which, in time, the soul of the lonely prisoner begins to emit, like the halo of a saint. Torn from the hustle-bustle of everyday life in so absolute a degree that even counting the passing minutes puts him intimately in touch with the Universe, the lonely prisoner has to have been purged of every imperfection, of everything that has stirred and troubled him in his former life, that has prevented his muddied waters from settling into transparency.[2]

Once again, we must not romanticize the privations and suffering, but it is quite astonishing that Solzhenitsyn should speak here of the prisoner who has entered a new level of freedom. Indeed his family and friends on the outside who try to maintain some vestige of his old life do him a great disservice:

> . . . a poisoned gift, because it transforms you from a free though hungry person into one who is anxious and cowardly, and it deprives you of that newly dawning enlightenment, that toughening resolve, which are all you need for your descent into the abyss. Oh, wise Gospel saying about the camel and the eye of the needle! These material things will keep you from entering the heavenly kingdom of the liberated spirit.[3]

Solzhenitsyn speaks as a man who having lost the world has gained his soul. This was certainly not the intention of his captors and tormentors, but in the mystery of things this is the result.

> Only my spirit and my conscience remain precious and important to me. Confronted by such a prisoner, the interrogation will tremble. Only the man who has renounced everything can win that victory.[4]

Ecce homo: behold the man! Jesus stood before his captors as such a man. Not as someone who had lost his freedom, but as one who had exercised it well.

It is strange, perhaps tragic that this mystery has been concealed from the church for most of its history. Very often the church has seen its responsibilities to lie in the legitimation of the political and economic order of the day. In Scotland, in Edinburgh as much as anywhere, it has traditionally sought to exercise control over social mores which in retrospect look to be culture relative rather than of the essence of religion. There have been notable exceptions, but they have been just that. Who would have thought that the foundations of the church lay in an arrest and trial? Soon in Acts when the apostles were in turn arrested and beaten they associated this with the experience of Jesus: they rejoiced 'that they were counted worthy to suffer dishonour for the name' (5.41). Then Stephen was stoned to death, and Paul later almost shared the same fate. The literature of the early church shows being arrested to have been quite common: condemnation and punishment were in turn associated with the sufferings of Christ. 'We must obey God rather than men' (Acts 5.29).

In the modern world this position has been recovered. In the providence of God it may well have been given to the church as a gift from outside. It is said that Mahatma Gandhi was much influenced by the example of Jesus, even in South Africa where as elsewhere the authority of Christ had been used to support civil and political order. Gandhi could see in Jesus a witness to the truth. Martin Luther King, Jnr, was in turn influenced by Gandhi as a witness to the truth. And now to complete the circle, the Revd Allan Boesak, one of the leaders of the black movement in South Africa, acknowledges his indebtedness to Dr King. From the time of the Civil Rights campaign in the USA it has become common for Christians to be arrested and to suffer for what they see to be the truth. As prisoners of conscience they have been free men and women, the rightness of their cause has condemned the judgment against them. They the accused have by their testimony placed authorities in the dock. Robert Runcie, Archbishop of Canterbury since 1980, will in 1991 resign and hand over to his successor. Initial assessments of his decade, which has largely coincided with the Thatcher period, have focussed on the regular confrontations between church and state, more particularly the Anglican Church and the Conservative Party. The fact that these should have taken place even under the primacy of Robert Runcie is an indication of the profound influence on the church of the picture of Jesus arrested, Jesus the prisoner, Jesus the witness to the truth. It is not primarily a political, but a spiritual rediscovery.

When we hear of prisoners of conscience our hearts go out to them in their suffering and above all in their loss of freedom. But perhaps we have got this the wrong way round. In *The First Circle* Solzhenitsyn writes of those outside who have their freedom and have squandered it in 'pettiness and vanity'. 'They lacked the immortal souls which prisoners earned through their endless years in prison . . . '[5] In the early church there was a clear distinction: Christians must not seek arrest, but when their allegiance to Christ became an issue, they must not shrink from it. It is only human to wish to retain social freedom and Solzhenitsyn notes that 'Christ in the Garden of Gethsemane, though he knew that he must drink the bitter cup to its dregs, continued to hope and pray.'[6] But he would not be free till he stood in front of his captors, never vindicated till he judged his judges.

2

The Scandal of the Cross

(*a*) *Political trial*

We have considered the trial of Jesus before the Sanhedrin. This was the first trial, Jewish and religious. It was followed by a second trial, Roman and political. Jesus was condemned at the first trial on a charge of blasphemy, probably because he represented an authority which condemned the authorities. But such a religious, in-house charge would be of no concern to the Roman governor. He was responsible for maintaining the peace of this Roman colony and its continued submission to Rome. He would only take action if the charge was that the prisoner was a threat to the peace, if he was the focus of a rebellious movement against the empire. Jesus was therefore brought before Pilate as a messianic pretender.

Until recently this might all have seemed rather remote, but at the present time blasphemy and the criminal law has become an emotive issue. It transpires that although many Muslims consider Salman Rushdie's *The Satanic Verses* to be blasphemous, the law of blasphemy in Britain applies only to the Christian religion. The debate has now focussed on whether the law should be extended to include Islam (and other religions), or whether it should be abolished altogether. I have no doubt it should be abolished. Religion neither can nor needs to be defended by law, but it can be compromised by the protection of the law. The German romantic poet of the last century, Heinrich Heine, commenting on the situation in his own time, observed that the Prussian police preferred people to believe in God since 'whoever tears himself away from his God will sooner or later break with his earthly superiors too'.[1] The original motivation in formulating the law of blasphemy was to ensure the continued status of religion in society, and thus the religious legitimation of the state. Such protection is unnecessary, and comes at too high a price. Although Pilate had no interest in blasphemy, he recognized the danger to the empire of anyone who publicly criticized the representatives of religious authority.

The trial before Pilate is no less confusing in its own way: indeed it was not really a trial at all. It is even less likely that any of the immediate followers of Jesus was present at these proceedings. There has been some dispute amongst scholars as to whether the Sanhedrin at that period had the authority to execute. Our information is incomplete on the matter, but the fact that within a few years at most Stephen could be condemned to death by stoning would indicate that the Sanhedrin had the authority to carry out the sentence of death against Jesus. We are told that at the time of the Passover there was indeed a plot against Jesus: 'And the chief priests and the scribes were seeking how to arrest him by stealth and kill him; for they said, "Not during the feast, lest there be a tumult of the people" ' (Mark 14.1–2). This would indicate that the Sanhedrin could condemn and execute Jesus, and that they had no scruple about doing it during the feast. The impediment was practical rather than legal: Jesus had considerable popular support. For this reason Jesus' enemies arranged to have him condemned and executed by the Romans.

There is an important point at issue here, since there is an inconsistency in the story. At one point in the trial before Pilate the crowd are reported as turning against Jesus, willing to see him crucified. If it had been so easy to turn the crowd against Jesus, then the Sanhedrin could have proceeded to have Jesus executed by stoning. When we recall that Jesus was arrested at night, secretly, tried with haste and then taken directly to Pilate another scenario suggests itself. The crowd may never have turned against Jesus, but instead may have arisen that morning to find that the Romans had condemned yet another of their popular leaders. The church has presented the broader picture that not only the leaders, but all of the Jews rejected Jesus and acquiesced in his crucifixion. This became a matter of dogma but may not have been true historically. This would be all the more tragic if it has contributed to Christian anti-semitism throughout European history.

But to return to our main theme; the Jewish authorities handed Jesus over to Pilate to be condemned and executed, this time under Roman law. We have observed that the trial before the Sanhedrin was guided by the church's attempt to present Jesus as a man entirely innocent under religious law, condemned because of the bad faith of the religious authorities. So now in the trial before Pilate Jesus is portrayed as entirely innocent under political law, as if he were of no political significance whatsoever. The political trial is very convoluted indeed:

1. There is first of all Matthew's account. Pilate questioned Jesus but found no reason to condemn him. He knew that it was because of envy that Jesus had been brought before him. But instead of simply releasing him, he attempted a diplomatic move. If Jesus could be the prisoner released in the annual amnesty then Pilate would have complied with the demand of the Sanhedrin, without actually having to execute Jesus.

2. According to Matthew Pilate's wife had learned in a dream that Jesus was a righteous man and advised her husband not to condemn him. In the Roman world dreams were regarded as a highly reliable source of communication from the gods.

3. And finally Pilate performed that action which has been associated with him throughout history: he washed his hands of the affair. The responsibility for the death of Jesus now passed to the Jewish people. The Romans who were entirely responsible for the death of Jesus are now exonerated. The Jewish people, who may well have been entirely innocent in the matter have gone down in history as being blood-thirsty and fickle Christ-killers.

4. Luke adds a further twist to the story. Although the trial took place in Judaea, and therefore within the jurisdiction of Pilate, Jesus was a Galilean, and Galilee was a self-governing province under the rule of Herod Antipas. In order to pass the buck Pilate sent Jesus to Herod. But although Herod abused Jesus he did not find him guilty of any crime. As so often happens this common problem provided a basis for friendship and co-operation between Herod and Pilate (Luke 23.12).

5. Luke confirms that while before the Sanhedrin the evidence related to the fact that Jesus spoke of the destruction of the temple, before Pilate the incident of whether or not to pay taxes to Caesar was mentioned.

6. But it is in John's Gospel that Pilate's attempts to avoid condemning Jesus go on longest. Pilate first of all refused to try Jesus at all. He then entered into a dialogue with Jesus, culminating with the famous question, 'What is truth?' Even after Jesus was scourged Pilate still wished to release him. On hearing that Jesus

was called the Son of God Pilate wished to know his origins. He was insistent that he should release Jesus. But the Jewish leaders took the ultimate step and threatened Pilate. 'If you release this man, you are not Caesar's friend . . . ' (John 19.12). That was too much for Pilate and he handed Jesus over for crucifixion.

(*b*) *Pilate in history*

In this convoluted sequence Pilate is presented as an essentially fair but weak man, one who had moral and even religious sensibilities, but was just incapable of decisive action. That is how he is remembered in Christian history. Nothing, however, could be further from the truth. The Jewish historian Josephus, writing during the first century AD, recounts two incidents from the life of Pilate. The first was when he ordered the imperial standards to be carried by his troops into Jerusalem, tantamount to introducing pagan images. When confronted by threat of civil disorder he withdrew the standards. In the second incident Jews were protesting about the fact that Pilate had used temple funds to pay for the building of aqueducts. He secretly ordered troops to infiltrate the crowds and then to attack them on a signal. Pilate was not a fair but weak man. In the year 39 AD the philosopher Philo, a leader of the Jewish community in Alexandria, led an embassy to the emperor Caligula to complain about the persecution of Jews in the city which took place with at least the tacit approval of the governor Flaccus. In his account of the proceedings, *Legatio ad Gaium*, he cites the case of another governor, Pontius Pilate. Recounting the incident of the insignia carried into Jerusalem, Philo comments on Pilate's response to the objections by the Jews in Jerusalem: he, 'naturally inflexible, a blend of self-will and relentlessness, stubbornly refused . . . ' The Jews then threatened to write to Tiberius, convinced that the emperor would not approve of what was being done in his name. Pilate was 'exasperated' by this, fearing that this approach 'would also expose the rest of his conduct as governor by stating in full the briberies, the insults, the robberies, the outrages and wanton injuries, the executions without trial constantly repeated, the ceaseless and supremely grievous cruelty. So with all his vindictiveness and furious temper, he was in a difficult position.'[2] It is not difficult to see why once Jesus was brought before Pilate he was quickly condemned to death. Pilate was clearly not a man to let scruples stand in the way of maintaining peace in his province. He was also susceptible to pressure from the Jewish authorities, who might threaten to write that Pilate was no friend of Caesar.

In order to place the blame entirely on the Jewish people it was necessary to represent Pilate as an essentially fair but weak man. In reality he was a cruel and vindictive man only too willing to believe that Jesus was a threat if not to Rome then to Pilate's own situation. When the Sanhedrin brought Jesus to Pilate, crucifixion was the only possible outcome. And did Herod Antipas become friends with such a man? Herod, who is represented in *Jesus Christ Superstar* as an exponent of the soft shoe shuffle, whom Jesus called a 'fox' (Luke 13.32), was a survivor. He was a son of Herod the Great. When the same historian Josephus tried to find something favourable to say about Herod the Great all he could manage was a certain even-handedness: 'A man he was of great barbarity towards all men equally . . . '[3] He killed off his sons, whom he had named as his heirs. Indeed there was a saying that, Jewish king that he was, it was safer to be one of his swine than one of his sons. Herod Antipas was a survivor and had one of the most able teachers in the ancient world. We have seen that Jesus stood over against the religious authorities, who were capable of plotting his death. He also stood over against this political alliance of psychotic butchers. Let us not think for a moment that the world in which Jesus lived was a romantic place in which it was easy to love your enemies.

(*c*) *Crucifixion*

Of one thing we can be sure: crucifixion does not mean to us what it meant to people in the ancient world. We live in a society which has rejected capital punishment. It is regularly debated in parliament, or at least the same fixed positions are rehearsed from time to time. Capital punishment, we are told, is a deterrent against murder. Alternatively we are told that statistics in this and other comparable countries disprove this very point. Both sides are in danger of missing the essential issue. Regardless of the deterrent argument our society is not prepared to kill its own members. In this regard we have taken a step which distances us from the ancient world. But more than that, even those who wish to reintroduce the death penalty are speaking of a method of execution which is quick and in itself painless. Crucifixion was devised for the very opposite purpose. It was regarded with horror and often disgust even in the societies which licensed it. Far from being quick and efficient, crucifixion was not in itself a method of execution. It was invariably preceded by flogging, often accompanied by other forms of torture and mutilation. The victim was then crucified, to die a lingering death from these injuries and from the exposure and deprivation of being suspended on the cross. And if anything further need be added, it is that crucifixion was a public spectacle, *pour encourager les autres*, to terrorize all who observed it. For these reasons crucifixion does not mean to us what it meant to people in the ancient world. It is shocking to us and incredible. But in the ancient world it was terrifying and very real, because it could happen to anyone.

Crucifixion was practised throughout the ancient world from India to Spain, and even among the Celts. It was an expression of barbarism but it was also extensively used in societies which in other respects exhibited high cultural and civic development. It is well attested in our sources from the Roman empire. This empire jealously guarded the rights and privileges of its citizens. But then the citizens were a tiny minority of its population. Within its boundaries most people were either slaves or conquered subjects. We shall have a rather idealized picture of life in the empire if we attend only to the experiences of the elite whose accounts of their own lives have come down to us. Their privileged lives depended on the subjugation of the majority, and in the final analysis that was maintained by terror.

Crucifixion was not only widespread, but frequently practised. Yet it was seldom used on citizens. If it came to it they normally retained some say in the manner of their execution, and no one would choose crucifixion over the quick sword or the poison cup. Occasionally it would be used on a citizen, if he were guilty of treason or some other crime against the state or the person of the emperor. Then it would be the instrument by which the sadism of the executioner and the fury of society would gain expression. And these features point us to the wider application of crucifixion. It was normally used in the subjugation of a people, to break their spirit. And it was also used against slaves if there was any suspicion of rebellion. When the rebellion of Spartacus failed, 6,000 rebel slaves were crucified along the Appian Way. In the political context it was the instrument associated with the oppressor. In the social sphere it retained the terror of arbitrariness. Any slave could be crucified at the whim of his master, or mistress.

Crucifixion was regarded with such horror in the ancient world that even when it is mentioned, it is only alluded to: it is never described in detail. Consequently the accounts in the Gospels of the crucifixion of Jesus remain one of the best sources of knowledge of crucifixion in ancient literature. It is significant that it is never given any positive interpretation. The cross had no symbolic power in Greek or Roman thought. Nor for that matter was it ever given a positive interpretation in Jewish thought. In the Hellenistic period it was used by the Jews. Alexander Jannaeus had eight hundred Pharisees crucified.[4] But it was associated with the prescribed form of execution in Deuteronomy:

> And if a man has committed a crime punishable by death and he is put to death, and you hang him on a tree, his body shall not remain all night upon the tree, but you shall bury him the same day, for a hanged man is accursed by God . . . (21.22–23).

Crucifixion was not employed by Jews during the Roman period: it was extensively used against them. Even so, it was never used as a symbol of martyrdom amongst the Jews.

(*d*) *Christ crucified*

In the history of Christian devotion attention has been focussed on the death of Jesus. Indeed it seems at times that more attention has been paid to the death than to the life. On Good Friday it is natural that our thoughts turn to the circumstances and the meaning of the death of Jesus, but it must not be divided off from the life of Jesus. The manner of his death followed from the manner of his life. There is also a devotional tradition which has concentrated on the meaning of that death, almost to the exclusion of the circumstances. There is here a real danger that far from saying more we end up by saying less. In the enthusiasm to pass on to its symbolic value we evacuate it of its historical reality. In seeing its wider significance for all, we ignore its particular meaning for Jesus. These are not alternatives, but unless we stop and take time to understand what happened once, then we shall not truly understand what happened once for all.

Humanist critics of religion often point to parallels in the teaching of the great religious leaders, themes common to different cultures and centuries. Indeed they can even include some philosophers and wise men not normally identified as religious teachers. But what has this to do with Christian faith? Jesus was of course a religious teacher, and the world would be a better place if those who call themselves by his name took his teaching to heart. But that is not Christian faith. Christians are not marked out as those who share the common moral observations of ancient sages. Indeed Paul presents his message not as the fulfilment of the wisdom of the ages, but its contradiction: ' . . . we preach Christ crucified, a stumbling block to Jews and folly to Gentiles . . . '(I Cor 1.23). Familiarity with this message should not disguise from us how shocking and incredible it must have sounded to all who first heard it. From what we have just seen to be the consistently negative associations of crucifixion this proclamation was certainly unique to the Christian faith.

No Jew of that time would demur at the claim that God was present in a righteous teacher, but it was deeply offensive to claim that God was present in one who was crucified. Crucifixion, as we have seen, had no positive interpretation. It represented not the blessing of God but the curse of God, not grace but disgrace. No Greek philosopher of the time would have dismissed the moral teaching of Jesus out of hand, but to claim that the truth of all things, the secret of the universe, was manifested in one who was executed on the cross was simply madness. Christian faith may be true or false, but let no one think it is just what everyone knows. As the opposite of what everyone knows it is either an unworthy scandal, sheerest nonsense – or it is the truth which God has revealed about himself which could not be invented or devised by the greatest minds.

Other critics of religion have suggested that it is basically wish-fulfilment. It is a longing for the Father; it is a projection of our deepest desires. Religion on such views is an easy way out of a difficult situation, a fantasy devised by those who cannot face reality. Of course there have been religions based on ancient myths and primordial events. They have told of never-never lands somewhere far away. They have distracted the mind from the sufferings of this time and place and sought comfort in flights of fantasy. But there is only one religion which directs our attention to an innocent man tortured to death. Many have longed for a father figure who would protect them against such evil. But this religion calls on people to be prepared to take up the same cross. Many have wished that life would be pleasant and fair, but this religion begins from suffering and injustice. Those who think that this religion is a longing and a wish, an opiate for inadequate people, have for their own reasons ignored the inescapable starting point: 'we preach Christ crucified'. Catch 22: only someone who was deeply neurotic could find wish-fulfilment in this religion. For sane people its truth must lie in some other direction.

To the Jews the claim that the crucified Jesus was the messiah was a scandal. Indeed on a cynical view of the Sanhedrin we might say that the most effective way of discrediting Jesus and all that he stood for was to have him crucified. A crucified messiah was blasphemy. The writer to the Hebrews reflects this view in speaking of Jesus who 'endured the cross, despising the shame . . . ' (Heb 12.2). By comparison Paul is more direct. He does not point to Jesus in spite of the cross, but precisely because of it. His preaching is of 'the word of the cross' (I Cor 1.18).

Nor would the word of the cross be any more attractive in the Gentile world. To those born citizens the cross was an obscenity, a necessary evil in order to preserve the empire against rebellion and dissolution. Those who had either bought their freedom at a high price or had it conferred upon them for some outstanding deed had at last managed to escape from the nightmare of its constant threat. No citizen, whether one born to that status or one who had by good fortune achieved it, would in his right mind exchange places with those still vulnerable to the threat of the cross. And no one in the ancient world who was liable to its threat would steadily walk towards it. Yet this is Paul's extraordinary claim. Paul does not proclaim Christ in spite of the cross but precisely through the cross. There is one who though he had high status, beyond the threat of crucifixion, yet gave up his privilege and became subject to its threat and to its reality.

> Have this mind among yourselves, which you have in Christ Jesus, who, though he was in the form of God, did not count equality with God a thing to be grasped, but emptied himself, taking the form of a servant, being born in the likeness of men. And being found in human form he humbled himself and became obedient unto death, even death on a cross (Phil 2.5–8).

What madness is this that a man of rank, in this case of supreme rank, should willingly become a *doulos*, a slave? What madness that such a man having become a slave should not adopt a low profile, a subservient demeanour. But beyond all that, what madness to proclaim the 'word of the cross', as if in this event there was revealed the reason of all things.

It was folly to the Gentiles. No one in the Roman empire was prepared for the word of the cross. Well, not quite. There was a group who found a way to reconcile the story about Jesus with their existing view of things. Scholars refer to them as the Docetists. We do not know anything about them, except this general approach they adopted. The name comes from the Greek word *dokein*, to seem. It is a word expressing a contrast. When we feel particularly shrewd or sophisticated we claim that we can see through a pretence. We can detect a sting, uncover a scam. We are not taken in by appearances. The Docetists could see beyond appearances: they knew that how things seem is not at all how they really are. They did not dismiss the word of the cross as blasphemy or madness. They did something much worse. They accepted it, but on their terms. Since – and here they began with their assumptions about what is real – since the messiah could not be crucified, Jesus the messiah could not really have died. Since – alternatively – the divine cannot suffer, that could not have really been Jesus on the cross. This was the first heresy to confront the church and there is evidence that the writers of the New Testament were already intent on combatting it as they told the Christian story. But just as the devil did not finish tempting Jesus, but merely awaited a further opportunity, so this first and most potentially damaging heresy has never been finally defeated. It is the first and the most persistent. It was a threat to the reality of gospel then, but it is no less a threat today. The reasons have changed, but the danger remains. Then it was because of assumptions which people brought from religious and metaphysical systems. And today it is the same. We are in great danger of ignoring the events in the life of Jesus, in favour of interpretations of these events. We are in danger of by-passing history and going straight to theology. In this way we never experience the scandal and folly of the cross: it is always explained for us in advance.

It is unfortunate that the critics of religion have not paid sufficient attention to the scandal and folly of the cross. But it would be tragic if Christians were somehow to miss the same point, to so garland it with metaphor and metaphysics that the wood is transmuted into silver, the nails into diamond studs. Unless we face the reality of the cross we shall not receive the realism of its revelation.

To found a religion on one who was crucified was not to point to a never-never-land, another time and place. It was to remind subject peoples and slaves alike of the fundamental reality of daily life. Today is Friday. Whether it will be Good Friday or not will depend on whether the cross has the last word, symbolizing as it does the world of injustice, cruelty, oppression, fear and despair. If Friday is to become in retrospect Good Friday there will have to be something more real, more profound and enduring than this.

3

Suffering and Redemption

(*a*) *Neurotic piety*

Friedrich Nietzsche, the fiercest of the nineteenth-century critics of religion, once declared that Christianity 'is the hatred of the senses, of the joys of the senses, of joy in general'.[1] Of course we are incensed by this and immediately rise to defend Christianity against such a charge. And was Nietzsche so much better, a neurotic figure who fell under the spell of the manic Wagner and the brooding Schopenhauer? In a competition for a good night out, I can imagine the winner of an evening with Nietzsche enquiring as to what the second prize might be instead. But whether Nietzsche knew much about the joys of the senses, and joy in general, only deflects from the more serious issue which he raises. Why is there a case to answer? Why has Christianity to be so No-saying? 'Thou shalt not!' I recall a cartoon about a New England Pilgrim settlement in which an upstanding member of the community and his wife came out of a tailor's shop to examine a dark charcoal grey cloth by daylight. It was not as black as the couple's clothes and the God-fearing man was complaining: Do you not have anything less frivolous? In Scotland there have been times when God had to be worshipped without stained glass or painting, without musical instruments or ornaments and certainly without clapping or embracing or movement. Leave it to professional footballers with designer stubble to hug and kiss each other in public. In religion we keep our feet on the floor and our hands to ourselves. I recall Sydney Carter, composer of 'Lord of the Dance', shaking his head at the sight of congregations standing in rigid rows singing his joyful foot-tapping hymn. We can have some sympathy with Nietzsche who said, 'I should only believe in a God who would know how to dance.'[2] The irony is compounded when we think of the solemn intoning of the Psalms of King David, who knew how to dance before the Lord. The Psalmist tells us that 'He who sits in the heavens laughs . . . ' (Ps 2.4). Would life not be more bearable if we knew that above it all and through it all God laughs at its daily absurdities? One of the joys of my life is that my son Colin and I share the same sense of humour, especially on observing the antics of the media or the pretentions of public figures. What a relief it would be, especially for those living alone, if they were able to turn to God and say, 'Did you see that!' What a comfort in time of trouble, but what a laugh!

'He who sits in the heavens laughs . . . ' One of the things which struck me about the statues of the gods of ancient Egypt was that some of them were smiling. What would be the point of having your own world if you could not enjoy it, if it were a complete drag every day and all day? And many of the statues of Gotama the Buddha smile at us as if enlightenment had brought not just serenity but pleasure. And that is the problem. Religion is supposed to bring contentment, assurance, serenity, joy – but not pleasure. For a number of years I used to do Epilogues for Anglia TV. It was difficult not to fall into the mould. For years afterwards I would be accosted by people in the area who would recount some joke which I had told in the course of an Epilogue. I thought viewing life from a religious perspective was good fun. Fun? Pleasure? The comedian Rikki Fulton has killed off the traditional Epilogue by his portrayal of the Rev. I.M. Jolly who begins his joyful message with a deep, deep sigh.

If Nietzsche is wrong in claiming that Christianity is hatred of joy, that its God can neither laugh nor dance, why is there a case to answer? Why is there such concentration on suffering? The answer is of course because of the suffering of Jesus. But on closer inspection this is not a reason at all. Why Christians have concentrated so much on the suffering of Jesus is itself part of the problem, not an explanation. Let me clarify this point. I speak without irreverence and without the least intention to shock or distress anyone, but consider this scenario. As we have recalled, the Roman empire executed its enemies by a most cruel and barbarous act – crucifixion – which not only caused great suffering, but was intended to cause great suffering. In Imperial Japan such enemies of the state would have been executed in an instant by a single sword stroke. Execution, just or unjust, but without suffering. And it is here that I want to raise the question, without irreverence. What if Jesus had been executed, justly or unjustly, without undue suffering? Why has the suffering of Jesus entered so deeply and so persistently into the life, and particularly the devotional life, of Christians? One of the great collections of Christian art is housed in the Escurial near Madrid. Here is the impression that it made on one visitor:

> What a pity it is that the labours of painting should have been so much employed on the shocking subjects of martyrology. Besides numberless pictures of the flagellation, crucifixion, and descent from the cross, we have Judith with the head of Holofernes, Herodias with the head of John the Baptist, Jael assassinating Sisera in his sleep, Peter writhing on the cross, Stephen battered with stones, Bartholemew flayed alive, and a hundred other pictures equally frightful, which can only serve to fill the mind with gloomy ideas, and encourage a spirit of religious fanaticism.[3]

The fact that Jesus suffered can hardly explain the place of suffering in Christian piety. Quite the reverse, the suffering of Jesus has been recalled in a setting which seems to come from elsewhere. If in this Good Friday meditation we recall the events of that last day, including the suffering of Jesus, it is so that these things may guide our faith. There is a real danger that in some matters the Christian tradition *since* then is liable to determine our reading of the events.

(*b*) *Suffering in all things*

One of the most striking elements in the creed is that Jesus 'suffered under Pontius Pilate'. A creed after all is a statement of faith, of religious beliefs. But this is a statement of historical fact. It was not a very significant fact for the Roman empire and therefore it went unrecorded, or at least no record of the event has come down to us from that source. A historical fact rather than a statement of faith or religious belief. And yet it was of extraordinary significance for Christians. Without for a moment seeking to minimize the horror of crucifixion we can say that the fact *that* Jesus suffered was infinitely more significant than the suffering, the extent of suffering or the degree of suffering which Jesus endured. That form of piety to which we have referred, which concentrates on the details of the suffering, on its intensity or duration, is in danger of distracting us from the more fundamental fact *that* Jesus suffered at all.

The earliest heresy within the Christian church was Docetism. The first threat was not the denial that Jesus was divine. In fact the earliest Christians did not believe that Jesus was divine. The earliest and most dangerous heresy was rather to deny that he was man, that he was truly human. In our own time and place it is difficult to persuade people that Jesus was divine, that God was incarnate in him. But in the ancient world every society had stories of gods who became men. Sometimes a god would take human form in order to test his people, sometimes to make love to a beautiful woman. The gods could walk the earth for many reasons, they could take human form and enjoy many experiences. But there was one litmus test which could be applied. Do you wish to know if this being who stands before you in human form is really a man, or a god in disguise? Then observe one thing: does he suffer in all things as we do.

To claim that God had walked the earth in human form would have caused no stir in the ancient world. To claim that he took human form in Jesus of Nazareth would not have been worth arguing about. But that was not what Christians asserted. Not that God took human form in Jesus, but that God was incarnate in a man, in a human life. The nineteenth-century Danish philosopher Søren Kierkegaard pictured a king who donned a peasant's cloak and sojourned with his people for a day. He walked the fields and visited the villages. But did that make him a peasant even for a day? No, as he made his way with royal bearing, his cloak flapping open to reveal the regal robes beneath, he was then what he always was, a king. Not for a moment did he suffer in all things as did the peasants. The suffering of Jesus was absolutely fundamental to Christian faith: *that* he suffered at all, not that he met his death in a particularly brutal way.

The suffering of Jesus has been viewed in two different ways in the Christian tradition, with important implications for religion in the modern world.

(*c*) *Atonement: metaphysical or historical*

Although Jesus predicted his own death he did not stress unduly the suffering which would attend it. What was important was the final confrontation between him and the religious authorities of the day. The voice of prophecy had all but died out in Judaism. It was briefly heard in the preaching of John the Baptist before he was murdered. Jesus stood in this prophetic tradition: he spoke with authority which the authorities refused to acknowledge, and soon he would share the same fate. But Jesus made no special point of the suffering he would endure. The early church took a different view, and it is for this reason that the last events in the life of Jesus are often referred to as the Passion, the Suffering. The suffering has taken on a place and significance that it did not have for Jesus himself.

There was in Judaism at that time a belief that the sufferings of an innocent person had value in the sight of God. This may go back to the Suffering Servant theme in Isaiah 53.

> Surely he has borne our grief
> and carried our sorrows;
> yet we esteemed him stricken,
> smitten by God, and afflicted.
> But he was wounded for our transgressions,
> he was bruised for our iniquities;
> upon him was the chastisement that made us whole;
> and with his stripes we are healed.

These words were written in the sixth-century BC and scholars are unable to agree on the identity of the Suffering Servant. Was he a particular person well known within the Jewish community in exile in Babylon? Or was the Servant the remnant of Judah itself, now a light to the Gentile nations? But for the early church there was no ambiguity: the Suffering Servant was Jesus himself. Details of the prophet's account recalled elements in the passion of Jesus.

> He was oppressed, and he was afflicted,
> yet he opened not his mouth . . .
> And they made his grave with the wicked . . .

But there is a danger here. The first Christians were Jews, and the Hebrew scriptures were also their sacred texts. They expected to be able to search the scriptures to find predictive prophecies about Jesus. In the first three chapters of Matthew we find such texts.

> Behold a virgin shall conceive and bear a son,
> and his name shall be called Emmanuel.

The original prophecy was about a time when after defeat and exile the people would once again name their children as testimony to their faith: God is with us.

> And you, O Bethlehem, in the land of Judah,
> are by no means least among the rulers of Judah;
> for from you shall come a ruler
> who will govern my people Israel.

This was Micah's prophecy that after foreign invasion and conquest, there would come a time when they would have their own ruler again from the ancient dynasty.

> Out of Egypt have I called my son.

This is not a prophecy at all, but a historical reference by Hosea to the Exodus, the release of Israel from bondage in Egypt.

> A voice was heard in Ramah,
> wailing and loud lamentation,
> Rachel weeping for her children . . .

The words concerning the slaughter of the innocents by Herod originally were spoken by Jeremiah in his message of hope; restoration after destruction.

These are some examples of prophecies which had a specific meaning in their own time and place, but which were applied to the story of Jesus. Such applications must have had a certain force of argument on other Jews, but there is a price. History does not repeat itself exactly and there is the risk that the life of Jesus is fitted into an already existing mould. So it is with the suffering of Jesus. As we have seen, it had its own historical meaning, its own significance in the life of Jesus. But by fitting Jesus into the role of the Suffering Servant the suffering and death of Jesus are given a very different meaning and significance.

> Yet it was the will of the Lord to bruise him;
> when he makes himself an offering for sin . . .

In taking over this model the early church replaced the historical meaning and significance of the suffering and death of Jesus with a theological or metaphysical meaning. It made perfect sense within Judaism, but it has become problematic for many people today – many of them within the church.

In ancient Judaism, with its daily sacrifices of animals in the temple cult, the theme of the sacrifice of the Suffering Servant made perfect sense. The Servant is an offering for sin. This theme is taken up in the New Testament where in Hebrews the imagery is pursued and Jesus is now a high priest in the order of the mysterious figure of Melchizedek. 'He has no need, like those high priests, to offer sacrifices daily, first for his own sins and then for those of the people; he did this once for all when he offered up himself (Heb. 7.27). Judaism on this understanding was primarily concerned with sin and atonement for sin. Since the symbolic action in the temple was repeated daily we may take it that this rite was regarded as of only temporary efficacy. But for the writer of Hebrews that has been overtaken qualitatively: 'For by a single offering he has perfected for all time those who are sanctified' (Heb. 10.14). There is only one sacrifice which has true and lasting efficacy, the blood and death of Jesus. In passing we might reflect on the irony that the central sacrament of the church, originally the Passover to the New Covenant, is often understood as a daily repetition of that temple sacrifice which Hebrews tells us neither can nor need be repeated.

The suffering and death of Jesus have been given a metaphysical meaning which they did not have for Jesus himself. How many Christians today truly understand this language? But the situation is more serious than that. Is it even compatible with the teaching of Jesus about the love and forgiveness of God? Jesus during his lifetime taught that God forgives the sinner who truly repents. Indeed it often seems that Jesus teaches that God has already forgiven the sin before the sinner repents. Repentance is not a condition: God does not withhold his love. But this is not the model of the Suffering Servant. In that passage the prophet tells us that God willed the suffering of the servant, and it is because of his suffering that the sins of the people are atoned for. But is this a Christian understanding of God? In the history of the church this view of the atonement has been expressed as a crude balance. On the one side are the entire sins of the world: on the other the sufferings of Jesus. It is for this reason that the sufferings of Jesus have attracted so much attention. Our salvation depends upon them. However much this model might have meant to converts from Judaism it has little force for people in our own day, inside as well as outside the church. My point, however, is that it has nothing to do with the teaching of Jesus, it perpetuates a pre-Christian view of God. And above all it distracts us from the real historical meaning and significance of the actual suffering and death of Jesus. Superficially the metaphysical theory looks to be more subtle: in reality it is less so. It looks to be more religious: in reality it is less Christian. As we have already observed, it is when we pay closest attention to the real experience of Jesus that the most profound religious significance is revealed.

(*d*) *Redemption and the poor*

Does this mean that we can no longer talk about redemption? If redemption involves a metaphysical balance between the sins of the world and the sufferings of Jesus, a trade off which is required before God forgives, then we can no longer speak in this way – should no longer speak in this way. Redemption is a very theological word, and yet like all such terms it was originally an ordinary secular word. In Greek society *apolutrosis* was a word used in the market place. There were instances of men and women who, either through their own actions or by no fault of their own, became slaves. It was then impossible for them to liberate themselves. But someone else could come along and buy them back, restore them to freedom, to do on their behalf what they could not achieve for themselves. We can see what a powerful image this was for the early church in speaking of the efficacy of the death of Jesus: 'In him we have redemption through his blood . . . ' (Eph. 1.7). Believers are bought back from the slavery of sin. But if today we are still to use the term redemption, then it must not be in this metaphysical sense, which depends on the acceptance of the metaphysical theory of atonement. If we can still speak of redemption then it must have a historical reference, first of all in the life of Jesus and second in the modern world. Indeed it is contemporary experience which challenges us to pursue this direct approach to the experience of Jesus. Unlikely though it may seem, as long as we remain within history and human experience, then it is not difficult to see the meaning of redemption. This term, which was originally applied to actions with important practical consequences, has been reappropriated to describe profound movements in the modern world.

In 1844 the young Karl Marx reflected on the oppression and injustices of life in Germany in the early years of the industrial revolution. The European democracies had followed a pattern where by a series of revolutions the grievances of one social class after another had been dealt with. Absolute monarchy had given way to a society in which the aristocracy had rights. Aristocracy had given way to a society in which the rights of the new middle class were enshrined. Gradually the old injustices had been dealt with until only one class was left, still oppressed. How was that class to be liberated? Of course the proletariat could have brought about a revolution in which it replaced its tormentors: the oppressed would become the oppressors. But that was not what Marx meant by liberation for the whole of society. He comes to the most extraordinary conclusion, claiming that the oppressed class 'can only redeem itself by a total redemption of humanity'[4] It is extraordinary because in an essay which includes the famous assertion that religion is 'the opiate of the people', he reverts at last to this religious image. Oppression cannot be ended by the oppressors, only by the oppressed. And the oppressed will overcome oppression by refusing to oppress others. The oppressed class will redeem the whole of society by bearing the ills of society and thus bringing them to an end. This solution comes not from politics but from religion. He was familiar with it, not from the atheistic writings of the Doctors' Club, but from his knowledge of the Bible. People understand very well what redemptive suffering means, as long as it is real suffering, suffering taking place in real lives in human history. The less metaphysical, the more historical, the more real and comprehensible is the idea of redemptive suffering.

Such thoughts from the young Karl Marx have been influential in the development of liberation theology in the last twenty years. It began in Latin America but it has been appropriated throughout the Third World. One reason why it is the Third World which has responded has been precisely that the mystery of Christ has been experienced to be more real in the historical as opposed to the metaphysical. In the Third World Jesus is understood as one who became a servant, a slave, one of the oppressed. He took his place with the poor and exploited against the rich and powerful. In the essay to which I have already referred, Marx described religion as 'an expression of real suffering and a protest against real suffering'.[5] During the centuries when European theology focussed on the sufferings of Jesus, and the subject dominated its art, the church was not obviously concerned about the real suffering of the poor. But now Jesus has been liberated from such a constricted view: he is seen to have shared the suffering of the poor. And if religion is, or should be 'a protest against real suffering', then the liberation movement in the church in Latin America has exposed and denounced injustice.

Because the European tradition has been to deal with the suffering of Jesus as part of an atonement theory, suffering has been reduced to an intellectual problem. How can suffering exist in a world created and governed by a loving God? But in the Third World suffering is not an intellectual problem, it is a moral problem. Not how can it be explained, but how can it be brought to an end. In such situations Christians seek not to interpret the world, but to change it. Suffering has its real, historical meaning, as it did in the life of Jesus.

In European Christianity the intellectual problem has sometimes taken the form: how can the righteous suffer? But this is not a historical approach either. Jesus suffered. And one of the recurring themes of the early church is that Christians must expect to suffer simply because they are followers of Jesus. In face of persecution Christians are advised to: 'rejoice in so far as you share Christ's sufferings' (I Peter 4.12). That was the meaning of their suffering, and it was not a problem. 'Indeed all who desire to live a godly life in Christ Jesus will be persecuted' (II Tim. 3.12). It is not just that the metaphysical interpretation obscures the meaning of the suffering of Jesus, it alienates us from him. There are signs in recent years that even in Europe this message has been recovered. 'Peace with God means conflict with the world.'[6]

I have been claiming that the redemptive value of suffering can be understood by those within the church when it is presented historically, but it is salutary that its meaning may be understood even more clearly by those outside the church. The idea of redemptive suffering came back into the church in Latin America from what at first sight looks like an unlikely direction, the Cuban revolution.

Fidel Castro was the leader who initiated the Cuban Revolution of 1959, but throughout Latin America Che Guevara was regarded as the soul of the revolution. During the armed struggle in the Sierra Maestra this doctor from Buenos Aires was the commander of the Second Column. He appears to have been a man entirely without interest in religion, which makes it all the more significant that he speaks of the revolution as 'the struggle of a people to redeem itself'.[7] Others may speak in materialist or purely economic terms, but for Guevara there was something more profound at stake as the people moved 'resolutely along the road to their redemption'.[8] Guevara knew that the oppressed throughout the continent looked to what was happening in Cuba: 'we constitute at this moment the hope of unredeemed America.'[9] No other term will do, but as he uses it redemption never loses its direct and immediate reference to contemporary events. After the revolution in Cuba Guevara determined to move on to assist in the liberation of Bolivia. Within two years he was dead, captured by the army, shot in a cell. The Cuban revolution has been represented in the West as materialist and atheist, yet for Guevara it was a true and historical redemption. Castro has been represented as an atheistic materialist, yet this graduate of a Jesuit college used very different words in a tribute to his fallen comrade. 'His blood was shed in Bolivia, for the redemption of the exploited and the oppressed.'[10] People know what sacrifice is about, they understand redemption by the shedding of blood – as long as these are matters of human experience, as long as they refer to human relations and not metaphysical transactions. The mystery of the redemption brought about by the suffering and death of Jesus is real when it is historical, when we look to Jesus himself on his way to the cross and to his death.

4

Women at the Cross

(*a*) *The disciples*

There is evidence even in the Christian Gospels that John the Baptist was the most significant religious figure of his day. He came from the desert and stood in the prophetic tradition of Elijah to denounce both king and religious establishment. He was a fearsome and fearless figure. He proclaimed God's coming judgment in terms which must have struck terror in his hearers: 'His winnowing fork is in his hand to clear his threshing floor, and to gather the wheat into his granary, but the chaff he will burn with unquenchable fire.' (Luke 3.17). To which Luke adds this laconic observation: 'So with many other exhortations he preached good news to the people.' This is the good news; John the Baptist on one of his lighter themes. And if he was hard on others he was hardest of all on himself, an ascetic who adopted the harshest discipline. John also had disciples. But who on earth would want to be a disciple of such a man? Confronted by such an alarming figure, fixed with his piercing stare, who would count it good news to be given the command: Follow me! Most would decline. (It is really most kind of you, and a great honour, but my wife is organizing a birthday party for one of the kids and I really must help with the hors d'oeuvres.) In fact it is more likely that John did not call disciples, but that some very special individuals responded to his message by following him. They were special individuals to take this step, special to share John's life, and of course special in their identification with him in his imprisonment and his murder.

John was arrested and imprisoned in the fortress of Machaerus by Herod Antipas. Anyone who is prepared to openly criticize the king is a threat to the state. And anyone who after his arrest is prepared to openly identify with him is in considerable danger.

Yet we know that the disciples of John went to him in prison and carried messages in and out. When he was murdered in the palace they did not turn or flee or hide, but went directly into the fortress to claim the body of their master and to perform that final act of bravery and loyalty. More remarkable than the story itself is the fact that it should be recorded for us in the Gospels, the literature of a rival sect. Remarkable because we cannot help but compare the disciples of John and the disciples of Jesus. When their master was arrested they fled. When he was in prison they hid. It was by his own that he was betrayed and by his own that he was denied. When it was finally over no disciple came to claim the body and perform that last act of loyalty and of love.

The disciples of John and of Jesus do not compare well, but that is not the only point of comparison. If John's disciples chose to follow him, Jesus also had his followers. Indeed there is a great contrast between the disciples of Jesus and these followers, in particular one category of follower. Firstly, they showed initiative in identifying with Jesus, while the disciples were called. Secondly, while the followers understood his message, the disciples are frequently presented as lacking religious insight, or even common sense: 'Jesus said to them, "Take heed and beware of the leaven of the Pharisees and Sadducees." And they discussed among themselves, saying, "We brought no bread"' (Matt 16.6–7). Thirdly, although the disciples fled and hid, these followers went with Jesus to the cross, and stayed with him till death, indeed accompanied his body to the tomb. And fourthly, as if these contrasts were not sufficiently striking, this group of followers were women.

(*b*) *Women followers*

In the history of the church much has been made of the disciples, whom Jesus specifically called to follow him. Yet they betrayed, denied and forsook him. To claim to stand in this apostolic tradition is an act of considerable humility. By comparison little has been made of the followers of Jesus, those who were not specifically called but who made their own decision. If anything we should think more of them for this, not less. They took the initiative in deciding, they were persistent in their following. Beyond that, many of them were women. We should not allow modern assumptions to disguise from us the significance of this fact. This was a movement to which many women committed themselves, in a society in which they were discourged from taking any initiatives, especially in matters of religion. The position might be summed up in the words of this daily prayer.

> Blessed be God that he has not made me a Gentile.
> Blessed be God that he has not made me a woman.[1]

As I was preparing these meditations the new chief rabbi for the UK, Dr Jonathan Saks, when questioned on the issue declined to say that women could be allowed to lead public prayer and give the blessing. This he claimed was a male role: women could pray in private. We should not think for a moment that it was automatic that many Jewish women would take the initiative and commit themselves to the Jesus movement.

From time to time it is observed that the majority of people in the church are women. Statistically this is so, indeed has probably always been so. The fact that the majority have traditionally had so little influence on the organization, liturgy, spirituality and theology of the church has its own significance. But it is not that to which I wish to draw attention. The observation that most Christians are and have been women is somehow assumed to be a criticism. It says something negative about the church and about Christian faith. Yet in the Gospels themselves the male disciples are portrayed as having neither religious insight nor moral courage. The women followers are portrayed as having both in considerable measure. On the evidence of the Gospels the conclusion is clear enough. There has been an imbalance of chiefs and Indians. The church has suffered from being dominated by disciples rather than guided by followers.

The ministry of Jesus attracted the loyalty and commitment of a broad cross-section of women. Nor is it difficult to see why it did. The Pharisees brought a woman to Jesus as he taught in the temple. As usual the suggestion is that they came not to learn but to entrap him. The woman was guilty of adultery and the law required that she be stoned to death. Of course Jesus had spoken specifically against adultery, adultery of the deed and adultery of the heart. But this did not lead him to give her over to the mob (John 8.2–11).[2] A second example is found in the case of the raising of the daughter of Jairus. By taking the child by the hand, if she were indeed dead, for her sake he would have become ritually unclean. And this in the house of the leader of the synagogue. Yet this he did not hesitate to do, and addressed her tenderly: 'talitha cumi' (Mark 5.41). This is one of a select number of Aramaic words and phrases embedded in the Greek text of the Gospels. Presumably they made a particular impact on the occasion they were spoken, and were recalled whenever the incident was recounted. A more colloquial translation suggested by the etymology is 'little lamb'. A third example is cleverly interposed within the same narrative. On his way to the house of Jairus Jesus was touched by a woman with a haemorrhage of blood. Because of this condition she would have been permanently unclean and therefore ostracized by society and prevented from living a normal life, through no fault of her own. Yet such was the reputation of Jesus that the woman trusted in him. Again, she is addressed tenderly, 'Daughter, your faith has made you well; go in peace, and be healed of your disease' (Mark 5.34).

In a fourth example the same compassion is shown to a mother, a widow from Nain. Jesus raised her son to life again. The crowd was amazed and we are told that 'fear seized them'. But in the midst of this commotion Jesus did not lose sight of the occasion of the miracle, the grief of the widow for her son, and Luke duly notes, 'he gave him to his mother'. Only then does the story end (Luke 7.11–15). The subject of our fifth example is also a woman, but a foreign woman. A devout Jew would not hold a conversation with a Syrophoenician let alone a Syrophoenician woman. She wished him to heal her daughter and Jesus as a matter of principle would not. Yet not only did the woman persist, but by turning Jesus' argument to her own advantage, she finally drew him into healing the little girl. A foreign woman and her little daughter were vulnerable in the ancient world, as in the modern, but Jesus came to their aid. This incident recalls what could be our sixth example, the encounter in Samaria when Jesus asked a woman to draw water for him from the well of Jacob. When his disciples arrived they were amazed that he was speaking to a woman at all – yet we are told that Jesus knew further what sort of woman she was. Even so, or precisely so, he spoke to her of life (John 4.7–30).

It is not surprising that women were drawn to Jesus for help, nor is it surprising that some should have been drawn to follow him as the great religious teacher of the day. Further illustrations appear in three curiously related incidents. In the first Luke tells us of a woman who came into the house of Simon the Pharisee where Jesus was a guest. She wet Jesus' feet with her tears, anointed them with oil, and then wiped his feet with her hair. The Pharisee was offended because she was a known sinner. But Jesus contrasted her devotion to him with the lack of welcome offered by his host. She knew how sinful she was and because of that she was all the more grateful for his assurance of God's forgiveness. The woman had more faith than the man, the laywoman more faith than the cleric. This is a familiar reversal found in the Gospels. In passing we might note that the scene depicts one of the most erotic actions in the Bible. If Jesus could suffer in all things as we do, we should hope that he could also enjoy things as we do. No doubt he took great pleasure in this action and might also have been aroused by it. Mark has what looks to be the same story, but it is placed in the house of Simon the leper, not Simon the Pharisee, and the place is given as Bethany. The oil is now poured over Jesus' head, and since the incident comes at the end of the Gospel, the meaning is the anointing of the body of Jesus. It is no longer an erotic action, but since it displays both devotion and insight, far beyond the capacity of the male disciples, Jesus says 'wherever the gospel is preached in the whole world, what she has done will be told in memory of her' (Mark 14.9). And who was she? We know the name of the betrayer of Jesus, the denier of Jesus and the names of the disciples who forsook him and fled. But because she was a woman, and in spite of the fact that she understood what the disciples could not understand, her name has been lost to the church and to its history.

The first incident took place in Luke 7, the second is found in Luke 10. Here in an unnamed village we meet two sisters, Mary and Martha. Martha takes the initiative in inviting Jesus into their home. No male member of the family is mentioned, yet Mary sits right there with the men to listen to the teaching of Jesus. Martha is busy preparing the welcoming meal. Mary is praised, but through the centuries women have identified with Martha, the one who had to give up the pleasure of joining the others, because someone has to get the dinner ready.

The third incident is recorded in John's Gospel, chapter 11. It deals with the raising of Lazarus from the dead. His home is Bethany, and his sisters are Mary and Martha. Mary is identified as the woman who wiped Jesus' feet with her hair. Are these the same Mary and Martha we met in Luke? Luke did not mention

Bethany in chapter 10, nor did he tell us that it was this same Mary he had described in chapter 7. We might have expected him to if this Mary was therefore the known sinner. John mentions it as an aside. How easily we make assumptions: how easily are reputations destroyed. But of one thing we can be absolutely sure. We are speaking here about Mary of Bethany and certainly not Mary Magdalene. She is mentioned only once in the four Gospels before the scenes at the cross. Luke tells us Jesus cured her of spirit possession. Yet in the most arbitrary way patristic writers simply assumed that Mary of Magdala was Mary of Bethany, was the known sinner. Poor Mary! There is absolutely no suggestion in any of the Gospels of wrong-doing, and yet she has been condemned through church history as a known sinner. How quickly are reputations destroyed, never to be restored. People are prepared to believe the worst on no evidence whatsoever: when asked to believe the best, they adopt a worldly-wise posture, and decline to be taken in.

(*c*) *Confession of faith*

How do you picture Martha? Is she a bustling, over-active figure concentrating on the work which has to be done? Is she somewhat overweight, wiping her hands on the corner of her apron, pushing away an unruly curl from her eye? It would not surprise you to know that she is 'the patroness of the cooks and housekeepers of Catholic clergy'![3] Where would we be without Martha? But how has it come to this? Such a picture is based on the incident in Luke – and completely ignores the much more important passage in John. It is worth reflecting on the account. In the style of the Fourth Gospel, the death of Lazarus is presented from the outset as an occasion when the presence of God and the glory of God will be manifest. It is as though Jesus waited to make sure that Lazarus was really dead. But he already knew what the outcome would be. Lazarus was not finally lost, but asleep. Now any child can see that this is a metaphor, but once again the male disciples of Jesus are presented as men of even less than average comprehension of such things. 'Lord, if he has fallen asleep, he will recover.' Or as the writer goes on to patiently explain in an aside to us: 'Now Jesus had spoken of his death, but they thought that he meant taking rest in sleep.' Jesus told them plainly what had happened, and why they were going to be with Lazarus. At which point Thomas blurted out: 'Let us also go, that we may die with him.' Frankly, this is embarrassing. They seem to understand nothing at all. What is the point of all this? The effect is certainly clear. We find a dramatic contrast between the disciples and Martha. Mary once again sat at home, but Martha took the initiative and went out to meet Jesus, and immediately expressed her confidence that although Lazarus was dead, God would grant whatever Jesus asked. Jesus began to tell her that Lazarus would rise again. In contrast to the disciples, who were capable of misunderstanding the most straightforward matters, Martha was never in any doubt about Jesus' meaning. She did indeed believe that there would be a general resurrection at the end of time. But in the theology of the Fourth Gospel, Jesus declared that this time had come.

> 'I am the resurrection and the life; he who believes in me, though he die, yet shall he live, and whoever lives and believes in me shall never die. Do you believe this?' She said to him, 'Yes, Lord: I believe that you are the Christ, the Son of God, he who is coming into the world.'

And this dramatic moment is the climax of the story. Of course we pay no attention to it. We rush on ahead to the tomb, to hear the call go out: Lazarus, come on down! We want to see Lazarus being summoned from the tomb, dazed, confused, stumbling into the light, untying the winding cloth from around his head. But Lazarus rose to die another day. The climax of the story is the confession of faith. 'Yes Lord: I believe that you are the Christ, the Son of God, he who is coming into the world.' In the other Gospels there is such a confession of faith. Matthew 16 contains one of the great controversial passages in the New Testament: '"But whom do you say that I am?" Simon Peter replied, "You are the Christ, Son of the living God."' And in receiving this confession Jesus addressed him as Peter: ' . . . and on this rock I will build my church, and the powers of death shall not prevail against it. I will give you the keys of the kingdom of heaven . . . ' But what does Martha get? The First Three Gospels have this confession of faith by Peter, but not the Fourth Gospel. In John's Gospel Peter says only 'We have believed, and have come to know, that you are the Holy One of God' (6.69). It is absolutely astonishing that the confession of faith that Jesus is the Christ is here made by a woman, by Martha the follower, not Peter the disciple. For such a confession Peter is revered in the history of the church as the figure brandishing the keys to the kingdom of heaven. Martha by comparison is pictured wearing a rather pretty apron.

(*d*) *To the death*

We should have these things in mind when we turn to the last events in Jesus' life. Two groups of women are mentioned. Crucifixion was a method of public execution, and the public turned out to see it. According to Luke 'there followed him a great multitude of the people, and of women who bewailed and lamented him' (Luke 23.27). It must seem to us obscene that the crowds should follow a man to spectate at his final agonies. It has all the marks of tabloid voyeurism. There is no suspicion here that they were in solidarity with one of their own against the cruelty of the imperial power. Nor did the professional wailers, for all their lamenting, really know how near they themselves were to disaster. Within the lifetime of their children the Romans would sack Jerusalem, destroy the temple and initiate that diaspora of the Jewish people, the consequences of which are still felt today. And so Jesus could turn on them: 'Daughters of Jerusalem, do not weep for me, but weep for yourselves and for your children.' We can imagine only too vividly this crowd milling around the execution site at Golgotha. One of my teachers defined *Schattenfreude* as follows: 'We can all bear other people's burdens rather well.' Far from being appalled, there is within us the capacity to view the downfall of another person with glee. It has nothing to do with what they deserve, but stems rather from a mixture of envy and guilty recognition of our own inadequacies in comparison. Without having to strike the blow ourselves, we are rid of such a damaging judgment.

The Gospel writers need not tell us of this crowd: their antics are all too familiar. There was, however, a second group of women. They stood discretely at some distance. The behaviour of the crowd would if anything have made their own distress even greater. In some complex way it would have increased the suffering of Jesus if he had to bear the taunts of the crowd in the presence of those who loved him.

Earlier I warned that it is easy to read the Gospel narratives from the perspective of Christian tradition. Given the history of celibacy there is a tendency to see Jesus as the leader of a little band of celibate men. Of course there were women in the background, Martha with her apron. But the story was essentially a male affair, the central actors were men. From this perspective we see that Jesus had been forsaken. He had been left alone, apart from the women. But who were these women, and why were they there? In Matthew we read:

> There were also many women there, looking from afar, who had followed Jesus from Galilee, ministering to him; among whom were Mary Magdalene and Mary the mother of James and Joseph, and the mother of the sons of Zebedee (27.55–6).

Mark has a slightly different list.

> There were also women looking on from afar, among whom were Mary Magdalene and Mary the mother of James the younger and of Joses, and Salome, who, when he was in Galilee, followed him, and ministered to him; and also many other women who came up with him to Jerusalem (15.40–1).

Indeed it is quite clear that there was a considerable number in this second group. They were not strangers and professional wailers. Nor did they happen to be in Jerusalem for the Passover. The group surrounding Jesus was much larger than the twelve male disciples. Nor were they lately come. They had been with him since the original Galilean ministry. This puts a very different light on things. Jesus was by no means deserted and left alone. His loyal followers were still with him to the end. They could not prevent the torture and the execution, but they did what they could: they were there.

It would therefore be patronizing, in the most literal sense, to say that Jesus was left alone, apart from the women. To be without the betrayer, the denier and the forsakers was more than compensated for by the presence of the women followers. And why were they there? Once again the traditional assumptions lead us to think of a little band of grieving women, anachronistically wearing black dresses and cardigans. Having set aside their aprons, they shrouded their heads in black head-scarves. But this is not the picture of women in the Gospels. As we have seen again and again the women understood perfectly well what Jesus taught. Again and again the women showed initiative in seeking Jesus out. It was the women who knew the deep spiritual things, and it was from a woman that the confession of faith came in that most spiritual of Gospels. They were not at the cross because they did not know any better, but because in comparison with the disciples, they did know better.

It may be that the Romans would not have crucified women followers of Jesus, but let us not think for a moment that the soldiers who had so cruelly abused and tortured Jesus would show respect for these women. Precisely by being there but standing apart from the crowd the women identified themselves and were at considerable risk. If attacked and raped they certainly would not have received any support from the Sanhedrin which had just handed Jesus over to the Romans. Nor could they have appealed to Pilate whose character was such that he was likely to take the part of his soldiers. We know how the testimony of the centurion would have begun at such an enquiry. 'Well, they were asking for it, weren't they.' Peter the rock and the other disciples were cowering in fear behind locked doors. It was on their own initiative and at great personal risk that the women continued to follow Jesus, to the death. They were a mixed group: some young, some with grown-up families. Can you imagine the embarrassment. While James and John hid in fear and trembling, their mother followed Jesus to Golgotha and stood by him to the end. How could they ever face her again?

But there is one final incident which we must consider. The disciples of John went openly into the fortress of Machaerus to claim their master's body. None of the disciples of Jesus was so brave. It was left to Joseph of Arimathea to do this. He was a rich man presumably of sufficient standing that he could do this with some confidence of immunity, but it was still a brave action. For whatever reason the women could not take this initiative. He took the body of Jesus, wrapped it in a shroud and laid the body in a new tomb, one which he had prepared for himself. We can imagine him performing this charitable action, perhaps with the assistance of some servants. As the shadows lengthened the task was complete. They rolled a large stone against the mouth of the tomb. For a moment they stood back, satisfied with their work, and then went home. It was a lonely place, but they were not quite alone. The women were there, of course! They could not claim the body, nor if they could did they have such a tomb at their disposal. But it is quite clear that this did not mean they yielded responsibility to this man at the fringe of the followers of Jesus.

> . . . and he rolled a great stone to the door of the tomb, and departed. Mary Magdalene and the other Mary were there, sitting opposite the sepulchre (Matt. 27.60–61).

The sequence of events had run its course, one traumatic shock after another, each more horrible than the last. Now the commotion and noise were over and there fell the stillness of the grave. The time of danger was passed. The time of tears now gone. Suddenly they are exhausted. It has been a long day. The longest day of their lives, and the blackest. But as darkness fell over them, over their lives and over the world, the body of Jesus was in good hands. By default the initiative and responsibility had fallen to them. When God's sabbath was over they would return to perform the last rites to his story.

5

Death and Dereliction

(*a*) *Bring back death*

I have said several times that Docetism was the greatest danger to the early church, and that it still persists today. It is seen in the pious attitude that protects Jesus against being really human. He could suffer, but could not have a good time. It is seen most clearly in reflection on the death of Jesus. The early Docetics believed that it could not have been a real death. Jesus must have seemed to die. Some believed that another had been crucified in his place. No one would believe that today, and yet Docetism still continues. It cannot be admitted that Jesus could die like us: even if he died, the experience must have been very different. But this is not what we are told in the Gospels.

Three times in the Gospels Jesus predicted his death: 'Behold we are going up to Jerusalem; and the Son of man will be delivered to the chief priests and scribes and they will condemn him to death . . . ' (Matt. 20.18). Familiarity once again robs us of the impact of these words. Few people know in advance the time and place of their death, and if they did then they would take it as a warning. They would be somewhere else on that day. Jesus neither avoided the time nor place, but as we have seen was to a large extent in control of these events. But more than that, he lived his life as one who knew that he was to die.

This hardly seems to separate him off from everyone else: we must all die. And yet death is a taboo subject in our society. We must all die, but few people reflect on this fact. Society discourages us from discussing it. Death of course is always present in society, but in such a way that we do not reflect on our own death. It is reduced to statistics: infant mortality rates, car accident fatalities. It is reduced to disease. In the first university in which I taught one of my friends was the professor of pathology. One evening at dinner he was very excited about a seminar he had just had with his students. They discussed death. All his professional life he had dealt with the dead, with dead tissue, with causes of death, but apparently he had never reflected on death. Or again, death is reduced to criminal acts. Every evening on some TV programme or other a detective is solving a murder in thirty-five minutes. There is no lack of death in society, but it is always reduced to an object of study.

Indeed society does not like to call death by its name. Old soldiers never die, they only pass away. Like Ernest, we lose one parent and then another. It is almost thirty years since I was a patient in a New York hospital. No one ever died at St Luke's: they would CB instead. This code turned out to be 'ceased breathing'. The operation was successful, even although the patient died. High tech medicine manipulates the body: it is a battle between the surgeon and the illness. The patient has no part to play.

America has probably gone further than any other society in disguising the fact that death has come near. When driving through a small town the visitor typically approaches the centre along a pleasant tree-lined avenue, with desirable properties on either side. But he can see one house in particular which stands out from the rest. It might be a freshly painted clap-board two-storey family home, with well tended flower-beds and shrubs. It is of course the funeral parlour. The front rooms are just as they were when a family lived there. It is a place of life, not death. The deceased is laid out in an open coffin, and thanks to the art of the mortician his friends remark that he looks better than he has for many months.

Yet in recent years attitudes have been changing. 'Whose Death is it Anyway?' Does the patient not have the right to know that death is coming near? Must technology continue biological life when no human life remains? And if there is anything at all positive to emerge from the tragedy and suffering of AIDS it is the loving support given to many of those who are certainly going to die and who know it – many of whom have learned a new dignity in face of such humiliation and debilitation. When death can neither be denied nor ignored, recognizing it and reflecting upon it turns out to be very different from what society tells us. Before AIDS Irma Kurtz wrote these words:

> We need to have death back again. Its transcendence puts banalities, impotence, frustrations, vanities, and some kinds of love, in their place. Contemplation of terminal issues is not in the least morbid, but life-enhancing. I am not talking now about the soul or the hereafter.[1]

Contrary to what society warns, people are surprisingly eager to talk about death. It is not negative or morbid, but positive and life-enhancing. To be conscious of mortality can actually have a liberating effect on the way we live our lives. Jesus predicted his coming death three times. That tells us about the way he lived his life.

(*b*) *The Agony of Gethsemane*

We must bear this in mind as we turn to consider Jesus in Gethsemane. The evening started well enough with the Last Supper. Scholars have speculated that it was just that, the last in a series of meals which Jesus shared with his disciples. Jesus, surrounded by his followers and friends, sharing good company and good wine. I suspect that the atmosphere of these meals would be very different from a normal Holy Communion service. But the last supper, which the disciples would expect to be as pleasant as the others, was to be significant for very different reasons. They did not know it but the first step had already been taken which would lead Jesus to his death. Betrayal would be followed by forsaking and then by denying.

We have already considered the decision of Jesus to go out of the city to the Garden of Gethsemane. This would be reported by his betrayer and soon the servants of the Sanhedrin would come to arrest him. Nothing could be more striking than the contrast between the alertness of Jesus at this time, and the drowsiness of his followers. He had no thought of sleep, but sleep overtook them almost like a spell. Only three were taken with him to this special time of prayer. Jesus went on beyond them, and they fell asleep. Yet the narrative tells of private moments in great detail. It tells of the prayers of Jesus, quite unlike anything that we know from his life so far. These words in Matthew and Mark could hardly have been predicted. And yet there is a further passage peculiar to Luke and it is on this account that the Agony of Gethsemane is called the Agony. It is one of the most extraordinary passages in the Bible:

'And being in agony he prayed more earnestly; and his sweat became like great drops of blood falling down upon the ground' (Luke 22.44). Who could have predicted such a scene? For Docetism of course it was unreal. But if real, what does it mean? When Jesus contemplated death did he experience it as we humans do? And if in all things he was not less but more human than we, what was the experience which we have but which caused him such agony that it had a visible, physiological effect?

The Agony was caused directly by the prospect of death. Of course anyone would experience fear at the thought of crucifixion. We need not recount again the sequence of torture which accompanied it. But this is fear of the known. The Agony was fear of the unknown. Animals share our fear of the threatening, the known. But it is one of those features of human existence which distinguishes it from merely biological life that we have intuitions of the unknown, the mysterious, the awesome. It lies at the heart of religion. From it arise feelings of sublime rapture – but also of debilitating terror. It is not even the fear of hell-fire, for this too is fear of the known, at least the fear of something which has been elaborated in very specific imagery. No, the Agony arose from the unknown, from an experience which has nothing to do with sin, or guilt, judgment or punishment.

The Agony is seldom discussed in New Testament studies, or even in theology. Its implications are too alarming. The modern form of Docetism, which protects Jesus from being human, is simply bewildered by this incident in Gethsemane. But if we begin with Jesus as human, no, more truly human than we are, then we should expect him to have an experience in face of death which is acknowledged in the most profound examples of literature. It would be explored by great writers in all its breadth and depth in this secular sphere, without the false restrictions of an inadequate piety. Some might recall Dylan Thomas and the raging against the darkness: 'Do not go Gentle into that Good Night'. Like Nietzsche before him he affirms that life must have a meaning in its own terms, and not by reference to anything beyond death. But that is not the experience which gives rise to the Agony. It is found in one of the most famous works of English literature, *Hamlet: Prince of Denmark*. Shakespeare is now so famous that it seems to be regarded as being in poor taste to quote him. This is unfortunate, for two reasons. The first is that Shakespeare is not in fact very well known nowadays. His works could stand being rediscovered. The second is that even when his work is discussed, the issues he raises are not. There is a constant complaint by students that English literature as a discipline seems to have retreated into an aesthetic approach to literature. A writer feels deeply about some human situation, but when he or she is studied in English literature the subject of the play, poem, or novel is set aside in favour of how it is treated, the development of characterization. The actual subject which moved the writer to write in the first place is somehow regarded as being outside the field of English literature. In my experience this is the more so when the subject has religious significance.

The experience which gave rise to the Agony of Gethsemane is dealt with by Shakespeare in the famous soliloquy of Hamlet. The words are familiar, but when did you ever have the opportunity to discuss the experience which the words express?

> To be, or not to be: that is the question:
> . . . To die: to sleep;
> To sleep: perchance to dream: ay, there's the rub;
> For in that sleep of death what dreams may come
> When we have shuffled off this mortal coil, . . .
> . . . Who would fardels bear,
> To grunt and sweat under a weary life,
> But that the dread of something after death,
> The undiscovered country, from whose bourn
> No traveller returns, puzzles the will,
> And makes us rather bear those ills we have,
> Than fly to others that we know not of?[2]

Because of the influence of Christianity on the development of Western culture most people until very recently believed in a life after death. Indeed most people even today probably still have the vestiges of this belief. And yet it is quite unlike other beliefs which arise from experience, or can be tested against experience. The Agony arises from a fundamental aspect of human existence which is never completely eliminated by such a belief. There is fear of death, a basic biological response which on occasion actually assists us to save our lives when in danger. The fear of death is part of the biological will to survive. But that is not the experience of the Agony. It is not the fear of death, death as the end, death as the known. The experience of the Agony is, as Hamlet witnesses, the fear of a very different kind, the fear that death might not be the end. This is a fear which animals cannot have. It arises from man's capacity to envisage life after death, to anticipate life in the Kingdom of God. But the other side of that coin is the capacity to envisage a life after death which has no meaning, which is not human. Some religious people have naively pitied atheists who believe that all life ends at death. But for Hamlet that would be a great relief, if he could be assured that death was the end. The terror of the unknown, the source of Agony is that death might not be the end, and that life thereafter might not be human. That is an experience of terror which is completely debilitating, such as no experience of the world can be. It is the Docetism of false piety which denies that Jesus could have had such an experience, the only basis on which we can understand the physiological effects described in the Agony of Gethsemane? The words of Luke describing the Agony are among the most extraordinary in the Bible, but they prepare for the most extraordinary and incredible words of all, the Cry of Dereliction.

(*c*) *Alienation*

The Cry of Dereliction is incredible. Not that it cannot be believed, but that it could never have been predicted. The words were indeed spoken, but they fall outside the range of what we might normally accept as a matter of course. Although scholars have questioned the historical value of this or that word or incident in the Gospels, surely these words from the cross must be authentic. Who could possibly have attributed them to Jesus, if only because it would have seemed blasphemous to do so. They seem to be entirely out of character with what we know of Jesus. How did it come to this?

Docetists believed that Jesus was not human, not truly human. Stated just like that it seems too absurd to be a danger, but Docetism permeates our thinking. Yes, we believe that he could suffer, but are we equally open to the view that he could feel pleasure? Was he sexually roused by the woman who wiped his feet with her long hair? But above all, could he actually experience our alienation from God; Jesus who embodied the goodness and the power of God? If this seems unlikely it is probably because of this Docetic tendency to which I have referred, the reverend thought that Jesus must be human, but not too human. Yet there may be evidence in the Gospels that Jesus did experience human alienation from God in precisely these two areas.

First of all with regard to the goodness of God, what are we to make, for example, of his response to the greeting addressed to him by the Jewish ruler: ' "Good Teacher, what shall I do to inherit eternal life?" And Jesus said to him, "Why do you call me good? No one is good but God alone" ' (Luke 18.18–9). This saying comes after a scene in which little children were brought to Jesus to be blessed. He blessed them, but then had to leave the village to go on to another village or town. Every day he must have stopped blessing some children in order to go on to bless others. He must have walked past some sick people in order to reach others. If he did not finish speaking to one group he could not have gone on to speak to another. Making such choices is part of being human, choosing one good against another good, and choosing a greater good against a lesser good. Anyone who lives like this must experience the guilt not of evil but of finitude. Human life is a life of alienation from the perfect good. 'No one is good but God alone.'

But a second source of alienation concerns Jesus and the power of God. One of the greatest obstacles to our thinking of Jesus as a human being like ourselves is his miraculous powers. To anyone in the modern world reading the Gospels one of the striking features is the miraculous element. What would strike someone in the ancient world is probably the restraint shown by the Gospel writers. Compared with the later Christian works which were not given a place in the New Testament, the Gospels are very restrained. Jesus is not presented as a wonder-worker trying to overwhelm people by miraculous feats. Nevertheless they are there, the walking on the water, the healing of lepers. In the nineteenth-century they become something of an embarrassment to modern scholars, who tried to explain how they could have taken place. The Heidelberg scholar H.E.G. Paulus, for example, addressed himself to the walking on the water. He claimed that in the Sea of Galilee there are sand bars which run out to some distance from the shore, just beneath the surface of the water. And this was supposed to explain the walking on the water! To begin with it is unlikely that fishermen from that very area, as some of the disciples were, would be unaccustomed to such events. But more to the point, walking on a sand bar is not a miracle. Indeed it has no religious significance at all. Scientists would be less dogmatic today about what can and cannot happen in the natural world.

But I am not so much concerned with the historicity of individual miracles, as with Jesus' attitude towards these powers. Did he in fact experience them as something which divided him off from all other human beings? Quite to the contrary. His attitude was that everyone should have these powers. When Jesus returned to his disciples from the experience which is called the Transfiguration, he found that they had attempted, unsuccessfully, to heal a boy of epilepsy. Jesus was exasperated: not that they had attempted something that only he could do, but that they had failed to do it. When they asked him privately why they could not, the answer was that they lacked faith in God (Matt. 17.19–20). In other words these powers did not make Jesus less human, but more human. They were not the marks of a being who was other than human, but rather the marks of what being human should include. One of the most extraordinary statements in the Gospels is the commission which Jesus gave to his disciples as he sent them out to extend his ministry throughout the country: 'And preach as you go, saying, "The kingdom of heaven is at hand." Heal the sick, raise the dead, cleanse lepers, cast out demons' (Matt. 10.7–8).

Did you notice, or did familiarity disguise it from you? Jesus told his disciples – and don't forget to raise the dead. Did they? Could they? But at least these powers did not lead to any alienation. Rather it would seem as if these powers were the manifestation of being more truly human, the true life of faith. The faithful servant of God should always have such powers.

(*d*) *The Cry of Dereliction*

And this leads us now to two sayings from the passion narratives. The first is at the arrest in Gethsemane. Here is a confrontation of powers. On the one side Jesus and his disciples, on the other the soldiers of the high priest. Matthew describes them rather as a 'great crowd with swords and clubs' (Matt. 26.47). Now of course such confrontations take place before us daily in the cinema or on television. No child of this age is surprised that a dozen righteous men can dispose of a rabble of one hundred. This generation, warned against believing in religious miracles, is entirely receptive to victory against impossible odds, achieved through instant carnage, by karate or through disintegration by laser guns. Why did the authorities think that it would take so many to arrest one man? But this man had power to move mountains, to walk on the sea, to wither a bush, to raise the dead. Or in the words of Jesus himself: 'Do you think that I cannot appeal to my Father, and he will at once send me more than twelve legions of angels' (Matt. 26.53). But why not? Which would have been more surprising? The story might have been expected to continue that suddenly the angel of the Lord appeared in the sky above Jesus, wielding a fiery sword, and at that terrifying sight you could see nothing but heels, as the crowds scattered in confusion and fear. Would that have been more surprising than what actually happened? Who could have predicted that Jesus would simply allow himself to be arrested? What now of the power of God available to the man of faith?

The answer of course is in the prayer in Gethsemane.

> My Father, if it be possible, let this cup to pass from me; nevertheless, not as I will, but as thou wilt (Matt. 26.39).

> My Father, if this cannot pass unless I drink it, thy will be done (Matt. 26.42).

The final events are about to begin. Jesus sees ahead of him the arrest, the humiliation, the prolonged suffering, the jeering and rejection, the recriminations and the jealousy, the terrible crucifixion, the lingering path to death itself. And it is precisely as he enters this sequence that a final burden is imposed upon him. Now he experiences what perhaps he had never experienced before, alienation from God. Perhaps for the first time there is his will, and God's will and the two are not the same. And although he submits to God's will, it is not at all clear why he must accept this awful path. He who spent his life praying to God for others now experiences the alienation of unanswered prayer. The answer he wanted was not forthcoming. This is echoed on the cross itself by the taunts of the chief priests: 'He saved others; he cannot save himself' (Matt. 27.42).

As we have previously noted, the early church saw Jesus as the Suffering Servant of God, who in his human life actualized the vision of the prophet Isaiah.

> He was despised and rejected by men;
> a man of sorrows, and acquainted with grief . . .
> He was oppressed, and he was afflicted,

yet he opened not his mouth;
like a lamb that is led to the slaughter
and like a sheep that before its shearer is dumb
so he opened not his mouth . . . (Isa. 53.3,7)

If this is a mystery to the observer, how much more to the Servant himself, the righteous man who has trusted in God all his life? This dismay, yes and we must say also complaint, is expressed in the words of the Psalmist.

My God, my God, why has thou forsaken me?
Why art thou so far from helping me, from the words of my groaning?
O my God, I cry by day, but thou dost not answer;
and by night, but find no rest (Ps. 22.1–2).

The final scenes of the cross seem to be captured in the words of the same Psalm.

Yea, dogs are round about me;
a company of evildoers encircle me;
they have pierced my hands and feet –
I can count all my bones –
they stare and gloat over me;
they divide my garments among them,
and for my raiment they cast lots (Ps. 22.16–18).

The alienation from the will of God: why this cup, this way? The rejection by God: prayers are unanswered. The Cry of Dereliction is therefore not as incredible as it might first appear. Yet there is more and it is worse. When his disciples turned and fled at least God's will was being done. When his enemies triumphed at least God was with him. But now at the end, alone on the cross and close to death Jesus experienced a further alienation. Not just forsaken by his disciples and friends, but by God himself.

My God, My God, why has THOU forsaken me?

And the final alienation of all. Jesus taught his disciples to pray 'Abba, Father'. *Abba* is a baby word. It is the familiar, trusting, intimate address of the child. Daddy. It was so characteristic of Jesus that it was transmitted to the early church. According to Paul 'when we cry "Abba! Father!" it is the Spirit himself bearing witness with our spirit that we are children of God . . . ' (Rom. 8.15–16; cf. also Gal. 4.6). Although in Matthew in the prayer in Gethsemane Jesus uses the more formal word *pater*, Father, according to Mark even at this stage Jesus addresses God intimately; 'Abba, Father, all things are possible to thee; remove this cup from me; yet not what I will, but what thou wilt' (Mark 14.36).

If the Cry of Dereliction is surprising, shocking, we should not miss in it the most tragic alienation of all. Rejected and forsaken Jesus can no longer use the formal word Father. Worst of all, he can no longer use the intimate address: Abba. Imagine a baby born into a royal family. Like any other child he addresses his father as Daddy. What a shock when later, on state occasions he has to address the King as Your Majesty. But at least he knows that after the ceremony he can revert to the more intimate form. But what if something should come between them such that his father is no longer to him as a father, but as an autocratic monarch? What if it is not simply the word which is lost, but the reality of the relationship? This is the experience reflected in the last words which Jesus uttered as death overwhelmed him. 'Eli, Eli, lama sabachthani.' The alienation, the forsaking, the dereliction all expressed in this word. *Eli, Eli*. No longer Father, no longer Abba, but simply God: My God, why have you forsaken me?

6

We Had Hoped

(*a*) *Neither faith nor hope*

We have been meditating on a terrible sequence of events, but what would they amount to if Jesus all the time knew that this was not the end? The Docetists did not believe that Jesus really suffered, or that he really died. Who could seriously share that view today? But that is exactly the position we adopt if we assume that Jesus went to his death knowing that within a few hours all would be well again. This is the final danger of Docetism, to believe that the Agony of Gethsemane and the Cry of Dereliction were not real because a happy outcome was guaranteed. But if we begin with the evidence of the Gospels a very different picture emerges. They make it perfectly clear that with the death of Jesus all faith and hope among his disciples and followers also died.

Indeed we must say the same of Jesus himself. He had been converted by the preaching of John the Baptist and submitted to baptism. When the witness of this, the greatest prophet of the day, was brought to an end Jesus took up the mantle of John and came proclaiming the same message: the Kingdom of God is at hand. Jesus continued in this faith and hope throughout his public ministry, and communicated both faith and hope to his disciples. Left to ourselves we should say that Jesus maintained this faith and hope to the end, but that is not what the Gospel writers tell us. Instead we are confronted by the Agony of Gethsemane and the Cry of Dereliction. There is no hint of any faith or hope left. And if this seems harsh and unlikely, then we must say that Jesus went through the agony believing that God required it, although he himself could not see why it had to be so. But in the Cry of Dereliction we find that although he had kept faith with God, God apparently had not kept faith with him. Jesus on the cross was forsaken. He clearly was not anticipating a miraculous resolution.

That route had been closed. No legions of angels: no escape from death.

But what of predictions of the passion? I am sure they are historical. As we have already noted it would not take any inspiration to see that Jesus was on a collision course with the authorities, who wanted him dead. Added to each of these predictions of the passion is a reference to resurrection.

> From that time Jesus began to show his disciples that he must go to Jerusalem and suffer many things from the elders and chief priests and scribes and be killed, and on the third day be raised (Matt. 16.21).

But that is what it is – an addition. The Gospel writers, after the events had occurred, filled out the predictions with details about the Romans, and went on also to add the prediction of resurrection. In this they contradict their best evidence: Jesus himself went to his death without any belief that he would soon rise from the dead. That is the meaning of the Agony of Gethsemane and the Cry of Dereliction. If Jesus had any anticipation of a resurrection, it would have made the agony and the cry unreal.

(*b*) *Bad faiths and false hopes*

If Jesus did not anticipate resurrection, then neither did his disciples nor followers. At his death some were cowering behind locked doors for fear that they might share his fate, and all experienced disillusionment and despair. They were not waiting with eager anticipation for some reversal of Good Friday. They were not waiting at all. Luke tells us of two of them already leaving Jerusalem along the Emmaus road. They once had faith and hope in Jesus. They had left home and family to follow him. They had been with him in Jerusalem in the last days. And now they saw their faith and their hopes follow him to the rock tomb: 'But we had hoped that he was the one to redeem Israel' (Luke 24.21). We shall not understand Good Friday till we see just how black it was, and how many things ended right there.

Faith and hope died with Jesus on the cross. Perhaps we should make that plural: faiths and hopes, for different people hoped for different things from Jesus. Even after the first prediction of the passion, even after the hard words about taking up the cross to follow him, the disciples 'discussed with one another who was the greatest' (Mark 9.34). They had high hopes for themselves as a group, and individually. Take the case of James and John.

> Then the mother of the sons of Zebedee came up to him with her sons, and kneeling before him she asked him for something. And he said to her, 'What do you want?' She said to him, 'Command that these two sons of mine may sit, one at your right hand and one at your left, in your kingdom' (Matt. 20.20–11).

Some might think her the original pushy Jewish mother, but it does reflect a very specific faith and hope in Jesus. It is not surprising that such faith and hope died at the cross. Of course since then it has been possible to use Christianity to gain social status and political and economic power, but these distortions should not blind us to the fact that such maneouverings have nothing to do with faith in the crucified Christ. They belong rather with the values of those who crucified him.

It may seem surprising, but Judas Iscariot also had faith and hope in Jesus. The very name 'Judas' has become synonymous with one who betrays a trust. And to this is added the fact that Judas betrayed Jesus for money. 'Thirty pieces of silver' is likewise synonymous with blood money. Naturally Judas is demonized in the Gospels: there is a tendency to make him into a petty self-seeking character. Scholars have speculated that his nickname, Iscariot, might make him a political assassin, an urban guerrilla fighter. Was his hope simply to profit from association with Jesus, and when that hope faltered, at least to profit by betraying Jesus? Or did he believe that Jesus would in fact summon twelve legions of angels if a confrontation came about? Did he bring things to a head, and seeing things go terribly wrong immediately repent?

Peter too had faith and hope in Jesus. I have already referred to the famous passage in Matthew 16 where because of his confession of faith Peter is promised the keys of the Kingdom. Martha, you will remember, got a rather nice apron. But this is to run several things together. First of all Peter forsook Jesus and then specifically denied and deserted him. Peter at the death of Jesus was no rock on which to build a church. That part of the story comes later. But secondly, the faith and hope which Peter had during his time with Jesus were also dashed. That is why he too fled and hid. And what was this faith and hope which Peter had in Jesus? 'You are the Christ, the Son of the living God.' Now we know a good deal about the title Christ at that time. When things went badly for the nation the Jews looked to God to send a new king like David. The Messiah (Greek *Christos*) would be the anointed king of Israel and would by force of arms defeat their oppressors and rescue the nation. Since defeating the Romans was beyond the military capacity of any man, the Messiah would be a supernatural agent of God who would come with legions of angels. And Peter confessed that Jesus was the Messiah. But what kind of vocation was that? The Gospel text immediately goes on to the first prediction of the passion.

> From that time Jesus began to show his disciples that he must go to Jerusalem and suffer many things from the elders and chief priests and scribes, and be killed [and on the third day be raised].

I have already suggested that the reference to resurrection comes from a later time. Peter confesses Jesus to be the Messiah, and Jesus immediately goes on to predict his own suffering and death. What follows is of fundamental importance.

> And Peter took him and began to rebuke him, saying 'God forbid, Lord! This shall never happen to you.' But he turned and answered and said to Peter, 'Get behind me, Satan! You are a hindrance to me, for you are not on the side of God, but of men.'

But is Peter not correct? He has confessed that Jesus is the Christ, and it was well known that the Christ would neither suffer nor die. By contrast we know that whatever Jesus' vocation, it did not include the support of twelve legions of angels. Small wonder that the faith which Peter confessed died at the cross. This was apparently not the faith upon which the church would be built. We read that when Peter confessed that Jesus was the Christ, Jesus 'strictly charged the disciples to tell no one that he was the Christ'. It has always been assumed that Jesus accepted the title Christ, and swore his followers to secrecy. It is interesting that it is the same Greek verb, *epitimaw* which is translated here as 'strictly charged' and a few sentences later as 'began to rebuke'. Presumably they should have the same meaning. That is to say, Jesus rejected their faith in him as the Messiah, for he knew very well what they understood by that vocation. It did not lead to the cross and was therefore from Satan. The strength of his rebuke is an indication of the attraction of that other way.

(*c*) *Militant Messiah*

I have mentioned this point at length, not least because such a faith is ever present in the church. It is the second temptation.

> And the devil took him up and showed him all the kingdoms of the world in a moment of time, and said to him, 'To you I will give all this authority and their glory; for it has been delivered to me, and I give it to whom I will. If you, then, will worship me, it shall be yours' (Luke 4.5–7).

Jesus accepted that the world was controlled by evil powers. To serve the devil would have been a rejection of God's will. But would it not be a more subtle betrayal if he had become a Militant Messiah? To use the powers of this world even in God's name is to give evil the victory. This is a fine line which the church is always in danger of crossing. The Militant Messiah is the servant of Satan.

The same temptation may be appearing today in the unlikely setting of Latin American liberation theology. A recurring theme is Exodus. God defeats the powers of this world in order to deliver the oppressed. But is this Christian faith? In order to have his way does God kill the first born of Egypt, including the first born of the prisoners in the pharoah's political dungeons? Is the way of the legions, even the legions of angels, not the way of the world, which always gives victory to evil no matter the cause. If this is the way God rules the world then Jesus need not have died.

Indeed this has been the dominant tradition in the church since the fourth-century, since the time of Constantine the Great who made Christianity the state religion of the Roman empire. He was an outstanding administrator, an essentially just and honourable man, but he was before everything else a great military leader who unified the empire by force of arms. Eusebius, Bishop of Caesarea and the first great historian of the church, depicted the sovereign as the earthly counterpart of the Logos in heaven, a title given to Christ in the fourth Gospel.

> And this selfsame One would be the Governor of this entire cosmos, the One who is over all, through all, and in all, visible and invisible, the all-pervasive Logos of God, from whom and through whom bearing the image of the higher kingdom, the sovereign dear to God, in imitation of the Higher Power, directs the helm and set straight all things on earth.[1]

Whatever Constantine did on earth was hailed as God's will from heaven. He was God's agent, God's representative on earth. And from that time Christ was represented as a regal figure, embodying the imperial values. I was struck by this when in Leningrad a few years ago. I visited the old fortress at the heart of the mediaeval city, and went into the church dedicated to Peter and Paul. Legend tells that Peter followed Jesus to the cross, and of course Paul preached Christ crucified. And how is Christ represented within this Russian Orthodox church? To the right of the golden doors is the Christ icon. The painting must have been seen by thousands of Russians over the centuries, many poor peasants who could not read. As an icon it was more powerful to them than any written word. It pictures Christ sitting comfortably on a throne, wearing his robes. Or to be more accurate, wearing the robes of the Czar of all Russia. The message to the unlettered peasants, and to the grateful nobility would be perfectly clear. And did Jesus have to undergo the Agony of Gethsemane and the Cry of Dereliction in order to bring this religious truth to light? And is this Good News to the poor and the oppressed, that there is in heaven another czar, a Czar (Caesar) infinitely more powerful than his counterpart on earth? But even so just that, his counterpart. And is this proclamation what Paul meant by claiming that Christ crucified is folly to the world? Or is this not the fulfilment of the devil's greatest dream, a Militant Messiah who conquers the world through the ways of the world?

There were many faiths and many hopes pinned on Jesus during his lifetime, and all of them without exception were unworthy of his vocation. They died with him on the cross. It would be the greatest tragedy if they were to be revived in various forms within the church and given the revered accolade 'Christian'. If there is one value in this Good Friday meditation it is that we should reflect on this constant danger.

(*d*) *Increased in wisdom*

Although in the Agony of Gethsemane and the Cry of Dereliction it is clear that Jesus could not see how God's will was being done, yet he was faithful to the end. He did not depart from his vocation. No Militant Messiah, no servant of Satan. And here we come to the true mystery of the cross. How is the God of the universe revealed in the one who is crucified? Paul was in no doubt that this would be deeply offensive to religious sensibilities, entirely contrary to common sense: the scandal and folly of the crucified Christ. In his letter to the Philippians he depicts this figure in more detail, indeed the picture may not be originally Paul's and may go back to the earliest days of the church.

> Have this mind among yourselves, which you have in Christ Jesus, who, though he was in the form of God, did not count equality with God a thing to be grasped, but emptied himself, taking the form of a servant, being born in the likeness of men. And being found in human form he humbled himself and became obedient unto death, even death on a cross (Phil. 2.5–8).

It is a dramatic and courageous passage. It takes Docetism head on. It uses the language of that first and most persistent heresy – Jesus in the form of God, in the likeness of men – and yet it closes the door to Docetism. It affirms that Jesus was a real man and died a real death. But of course it says much more than that. What is the relationship between Jesus and God? If God is to be represented by Jesus on earth, certain attributes of God must be set aside. The word Paul uses, *kenosis*, means 'emptying', or more technically it means 'dieting'. Jesus is a slimmed down manifestation of God.

This has been a very powerful passage in Christian thought, but it has not been without danger, and as ever the main and continuing danger is Docetism. The tendency has been to think that Jesus set aside those divine attributes which could not be manifest in human life: omniscience, omnipresence, omnipotence. The human mind does not know everything, the individual cannot be everywhere at once, nor exercise absolute power. But this I fear is to fall into the Docetist trap for it is to affirm that God was not in fact manifest in Jesus as a man, as a slave, as the crucified. The omnipotent God could not be manifest in such a figure. But this is to entirely miss the revolution of the crucified Christ. The radical novelty, both scandal and folly, of the Gospel is that God is not manifest in the so-called divine attributes, the attributes which could only have been seen in the Militant Messiah, the servant of Satan. The radical novelty of the Gospel is that God is actually revealed in Jesus the slave, the crucified. God is not revealed in Jesus despite the crucifixion, but precisely because of it. He is not revealed in Jesus even although a servant, but fully and in no other way. The German theologian Jürgen Moltmann makes the point powerfully:

> God is not greater than he is in this humiliation. God is not more glorious than he is in this self-surrender. God is not more powerful than he is in this helplessness. God is not more divine than he is in this humanity.[2]

This is the scandal to religious sensibilities, the contradiction of common sense.

The great danger of this passage in Philippians is that we think the God who is already known is slimmed down, disguised in the form of Jesus, and then fully restored once again. But there is no new revelation here, nothing specifically Christian. The scandal and the folly arise because the Gospel is that the old God is dead. The pre-Christian God is no more. For Christians either God is as he is revealed in Jesus the crucified, or Jesus is simply a tragic figure. Either the cross of Christ transforms our understanding of God, or the cross was a mistake. The greatest danger of Docetism is that we believe God after the cross to be the same as God before the cross. If that were the case then the life and death of Jesus would be unreal and pointless.

Theologians seem to have spent more time considering the death of Jesus than his life. His teaching, his relationships, the community he formed, all of these things have been relegated to the less intellectually demanding sphere of 'practical theology'. And this has its own significance. But even when theologians have dealt with the death of Jesus it has not been his actual death and its significance for him, but its metaphysical significance in some cosmic plan. Such an approach falls into the trap already described. It assumes that God, already known, uses the death of Jesus in some way: as a sacrifice which atones for sin, as a payment which cancels debt. Thus the pre-Christian view of God persists. Nothing new is allowed to emerge from the life and death of Jesus. No new revelation of God is allowed to break through.

Now Christian faith might be true or false: it is faith and not some piece of objective data. It is the truth by which we might live, not simply information. But it stands or falls by this assertion, that God is definitively revealed in Jesus of Nazareth. This sounds familiar, but I believe its implications are so profound that we have never come to terms with them.

If Jesus is the Son of God, revelation of the invisible God, the manifestation in human form of the creator and sustainer of the universe, then the implications are revolutionary: a scandal to religious sensibilities and the contradiction of common sense.

If Jesus is the Son of God, if the Son is the image of his Father, that is to say the Father is disclosed as for the first time in the Son, then once and for all we must reject the God who rules the world through legions of angels. This is a pre-Christian, pagan God. Indeed we must declare ourselves atheists and unbelievers in such a God. This is the God of the philosophers, the God of the rulers of this earth and the deceit described in the Apocalypse as the dragon disguised as the lamb.

If Jesus is the Son of God, representative of God in his dealings with men, then we must dissociate ourselves from the Militant Messiah, servant of Satan.

If Jesus is the Son of God, then God's relationship to men and women is scandalous and incredible. It is expressed in the words of that other prisoner of conscience, Dietrich Bonhoeffer, writing not from the security of his study, but from a Gestapo cell:

> Jesus asked in Gethsemane, 'Could you not watch with me one hour?' That is a reversal of what the religious man expects from God. Man is summoned to share in God's sufferings at the hands of a godless world.[3]

'If Jesus is the Son of God.' The words are familiar. They are the devil's greeting to Jesus at the temptations, setting before him the role of Militant Messiah, Servant of the God who rules the world. In Matthew Jesus triumphs over the tempter once and for all, but in Luke the devil departs 'until an opportune time'. The words are familiar, but ominous too. In the final conflict these words are repeated: one final offer. 'If you are the Son of God, come down from the cross' (Matt. 27.40). But Jesus kept faith with God, even although at that moment God had forsaken him.

Throughout this meditation we have constantly confronted the temptation to Docetism. Here we face it in its most subtle and pious form, the temptation to think that everything was easy for Jesus, and perfectly clear. To the contrary, the evidence of the Gospels is that if Jesus lived by faith, he also had to grow in faith through the harsh experiences of life. At Christmas we read of the time and circumstances of his birth. But who gives a thought for the traumatic experience of being born in a byre among animals? And do we ever get as far as the end of the infancy narrative in

Luke? 'And Jesus increased in wisdom and stature, and in favour with God and man' (2.52). What a comfortable expression that is: 'to increase' suggests that the process of growth and development was without difficulty. The Greek verb *prokoptein*, however, was used of an army hacking its way forward through every kind of obstacle, and Barth tells us that in metal working it was 'to extend by blows, as a smith stretches metal by hammers'.[4] And in Hebrews we are told that 'Although he was a Son, he learned obedience through what he suffered . . . ' (Heb. 5.8). It is quite clear that Jesus not only lived by faith, but grew in faith. He kept faith with God even when he could not see why he must follow the way of the cross. If we say that something new is revealed in Jesus as the Son of God, it was not something that Jesus already knew in advance. That would be the final deceit of Docetism. Here is the real scandal to religious sensibilities: Jesus too had to experience the failure of a faith which looked to the God of legions of angels. No, Jesus' own faith was extended by blows so that through his suffering and death something new might arise, not something which the world already knew, but something which would be a scandal to religion and the contradiction of common sense, but which would be Good News to those who could hear it.

But here we are met on Good Friday. At this time on that original Friday nothing was clear. After the conflict, the strife, the horror, silence fell upon the women gazing at the tomb. The sabbath was about to begin when men and women must rest, and even the Lord God rested from the conflict of that holy week. Nothing had been decided. Nothing was clear. All faiths had been discredited. All hopes dashed. We have reached the end of the road and there is nothing left. Unless we reach this point we do not understand Good Friday. Along with the Docetists we do not believe Jesus descended into hell. We finish up halting between two ways. We hold back, trusting in old faiths and hopes which will surely fail.

And what are these two ways? The alternatives are stark. Was Jesus right in keeping to the path which led through the Agony of Gethsemane to the Cry of Dereliction? Or were his enemies right in representing him as mistaken, a threat to religion and society? Where is the truth about God and the world to be found? Is Jesus the Son of God or were his enemies right to reject him in order to worship the old God of this world? The two are in complete contrast, but at that moment Jesus lay in the tomb, his enemies rejoiced, his friends fled in disarray.

That is how the story ends. And if that is indeed the end of the story, then the cross of oppression and injustice casts its long shadow throughout the world in which we are condemned to live. Whether against all the odds and against all expectations, whether after bad faiths and false hopes this is not the end of the story, not the truth of all things, we must wait to see. Until the sabbath is over there is nothing that can be done but to watch and pray.

PART TWO

A Sabbath's Rest

Our Good Friday meditation ended in front of the rock tomb in which lay the body of Jesus. Joseph of Arimathea had gone home and the women sat staring, exhausted and dispirited. Since then the sabbath has come and gone. It is now the first day of the week and we await the arrival of the women. We are concealed from view, like parents watching their children wearily enter a room all unsuspecting, unaware of the surprise which there awaits them and which will soon transform their sadness into joy. However, we are a little early and there are some things we should reflect upon while we wait.

A few years ago I visited Egypt. Left to myself I should gladly have gone directly to the tomb of Amenophis II in the Valley of the Kings, close by Luxor, ancient Thebes. Instead I spent my first day in the Egyptian Museum in Cairo. My guide, a young scholar of Egyptian history, insisted on beginning with the geography of the land, followed by an outline of the various dynastic periods. Only then did we proceed to tour room after room of statues and artifacts from the mortuary rites of the ancient religion. I did not begin at the tomb, but when some time later I stood before it I understood why I was there, what I should see and what it all meant.

We took as a motto for our Good Friday meditations the thought that the mystery is *in* the events. We encounter the mystery when we attend closely to the events themselves rather than a theory about them. The events themselves were, unfortunately, not untypical of happenings in both ancient and modern times. There was the betrayal, denial and forsaking of the prisoner of conscience. There was the abuse of power, by both religious and political authorities. There was oppression, injustice and premature death. As we begin to meditate upon the Easter theme there is a clear contrast. The events described are like no other happenings in the ancient world, and they are certainly quite alien to our contemporary understanding of the world. Before we can discern the mystery *in* the events we shall have to consider what actually happened.

In the eighteenth-century scholars came to the conclusion that people who lived two thousand years earlier understood the world differently. The formation of consciousness, the processes of thought, the modes of expression characteristic of the ancient world were quite different from those of the modern world. This had important implications for the reading of ancient texts such as the Bible. Since that time there has been continual discussion of what we might loosely call the Easter events. The term Easter comes to us neither from Aramaic nor Greek. In mediaeval Europe it was the festival of the goddess Eastre, held in April. But its meaning has been entirely supplanted by the Christian festival. The events of Easter are discussed by scholars throughout the year, with erudition and subtlety. But with Easter morning the tabloid newspapers appear with row-over stories. There is always a row over what a bishop has said in his Easter sermon or in an interview. So far as the tabloids are concerned news has not yet reached them that there is a difference between first-century Palestine and twentieth-century Europe. Much of their reporting in the normal course of events is uncluttered by considerations of evidence and facts yet in this matter they claim to champion the cause of the ordinary punter in the pew – or not in the pew. Did it happen? Was the tomb empty?

These are questions which we shall consider shortly, but before we get too far into such matters we should make sure we do not lose sight of our goal. Christian faith involves Good Friday as well as Easter. We must not become so involved in contemporary questions that we set aside everything which we have examined up to this point. The mystery of Christian faith, is *in* the events of Good Friday as well as those of Easter. The mystery is not reducible to one issue, for example an empty tomb.

If the Good Friday meditation is filled with poignancy and a sense of tragedy, we have a right to expect that the Easter meditation should be one of joy and assurance. Yet some will approach this meditation with foreboding, considering that it will be concerned with controversy, difficulties and doubts. Not so. We proceeded in the Good Friday meditation step by step towards the most profound levels of the mystery. Now we shall proceed step by step towards the light, the disclosure of the mystery. Our subject is the origins and nature of the new faith, Christian faith. This is an exciting stage in our pilgrimage and we can approach it without any feelings of apprehension.

PART THREE

Good News

7

Metamorphosis

(*a*) *New men*

In the Good Friday meditation we referred a good deal to the disciples of Jesus, men revered in the memory of the church throughout the centuries, beyond our capacity to praise and certainly beyond all thought of criticism. If anything the opposite seems to be the case in the Gospel narratives themselves. Again and again the disciples are exposed as human, all too human figures. They have very recognizable faults and failings. Their behaviour is petty and unworthy. Indeed they get such a bad press in the Gospels that at last we cannot avoid the suspicion that this must be for a reason. It is not that they are criticized, not that they are shown to be lacking in insight. Rather it is that they are shown to be of less than average intelligence and religious understanding. Why are the Gospel writers prepared to present them in such a bad light? Two reasons suggest themselves.

The first is to make even more dramatic the change which they underwent. Then they were men of the old faith, bad faith and finally no faith. Now they are gripped by a new faith. Then they were entirely lacking in religious insight. Now they see what has happened clearly and understand its implications. Then they were dispirited, now they are inspired. Then they were fearful and fled, now they are bold and courageous. Then they were utterly dependent, now they are capable of initiative. When we ask what happened at Easter, this is our starting point. Metamorphosis, transformation, conversion, rebirth, new life. We are not speaking about something debateable, some metaphysical theory which can be understood by only a few and accepted by fewer still. When we ask about evidence, the disciples are the living testimony. In the eighteenth-century one of the first critical treatments of the Gospels was attempted by H.S. Reimarus. He claimed that the disciples had made up stories about Jesus, so that they could become leaders of a new movement and benefit from it. It was not much of a theory, but it begins at the wrong point. The most obvious of the Easter events is not what is said about Jesus, but the transformation in the lives of the disciples. If we wish to uncover and understand the mystery, we must begin not in what was said about Jesus, but with what happened to the disciples. The contrast is incredible, the more so because of the picture of them painted by the Gospel writers. This then might be the first reason why the evangelists write as they do.

The second is to focus on the power of these events. When Gideon faced the Midianites it was with as large and well prepared an army as he could muster. So much so that the victory would have been attributable to these factors alone. He was required by God to dismiss most of his troops, lest in victory he should conclude, 'My own hand has delivered me' (Judges 7.2). If the disciples had been men of religious genius our attention would have been focussed upon them. Instead it is made clear that since they had no ability of themselves, their new strength and insight, their new understanding and faith must be entirely the work of God, the revelation effected through his power. This could be a second reason. In the Gospels Jesus had a considerable reputation among the crowds, and with individuals of the ruling religious schools. But his disciples must have been something of a joke. They could not heal, they could not preach, they could not do any of the things associated with Jesus. Yet suddenly here they were. Jesus was gone, but who were these men speaking in his name? They looked like the disciples, but in every other respect they were new men.

(*b*) *Resolution*

How did they do it? How did they manage to change so radically and so quickly? But even as we ask such a question we know it will not do. Have you ever decided to change? Of course we can modify some aspects of our behaviour. For health reasons we might decide to take more exercise. It is a fine distinction but although we can easily change how we behave, we cannot so readily change who we are. Who is the person who is going to change not how we act but how we are? If our behaviour is a problem we can change it, but if we ourselves are the problem how do we begin?

One of the quaint customs associated with Hogmany is making resolutions. In the high spirits of the moment (literally) a woman might resolve to give up smoking, a man might resolve to be tidier around the house. The behaviour is at fault, the resolve is admirable. But we know what happens to resolutions. Some people find giving up smoking easy: they do it again and again. But what if the fault lies in the character of the person making the resolve, so that the resolve itself is flawed?

Martin Heidegger was the greatest European philosopher of the twentieth-century. His major work was carefully planned, systematically presented and densely argued. There could hardly be a greater contrast between it and Paul's Epistle to the Romans. The former a weighty tome, the latter but a letter. The one the considered product of years of thought, the other an immediate response to a practical situation. A philosophical text re-worked and polished in contrast to a pastoral piece dashed off as time permitted. They have little in common in style and even less in content. Yet both deal with this subject of resolve. Indeed Heidegger presents us with an existentialist analysis of the individual who comes to the turning point in his life. His true self appears when he resolves to live a new and authentic life. But for all his philosophical erudition Heidegger's proposition does not ring true to experience. For that we must turn to Paul.

> I do not understand my own actions. For I do not do what I want, but I do the very thing I hate . . .
>
> I can will what is right, but I cannot do it. For I do not do the good I want, but the evil I do not want is what I do (Rom 7.15, 18–9).

If our lives are flawed, our will and also our resolve, how can we change?

When therefore we ask how the disciples were able to change themselves so radically and profoundly, we already know that this is the wrong way to approach the matter. They did not decide to change themselves: they were changed. If they acted in different ways, it was because they had been acted upon. If they were able to begin a new life it was because they had been enabled. The transformation came not from will-power but from being empowered.

(*c*) *Empowerment*

It is perhaps inevitable that Heidegger the philosopher would assume that people's lives are changed by ideas, by understanding. And of course we do need to understand the situation in which we find ourselves. We have a will to meaning: things have to make sense to us. But that is very different from saying that our lives are changed by argument. I do not suppose that in European history there is a single case of a man or woman being argued into religious belief by a rational proof of the existence of God. Nor for that matter has anyone ever been argued out of belief. Arguments are appropriate at a certain stage either to make sense of our belief or our unbelief. Yet such has been the influence of philosophy on the development of Christianity that we assume people can simply decide to be religious, decide to accept the faith.

Only a philosopher in his study could take this view. The important things of life are established in no such way. Our faith in our parents, our love for our children, our commitment to the values by which we live: none of these things comes about by argument, though we can reflect on them. The profound things of life arise from experience, sometimes positive, enriching, sublime experience, sometimes terrible, destructive and utterly depressing. What is true for the profound things of life in general is of course true also in the particular case of religion. It is not a knowing, an argument about what is real. It is not a doing, subscribing to certain moral standards. It arises from experience but not simply having an experience. It arises from experience which changes us in ways that mere resolve cannot do. Indeed religious faith arises from experiences which move the goal-posts and set before us new possibilities we could not devise for ourselves.

But lest we fall into the philosopher's trap of speaking about how this must be, let us return to the disciples of Jesus, men whose lives were completely transformed. The conversion was not the result of argument, but experience. They were not convinced, but empowered. At first sight this might seem strange to us, we who think religion is about beliefs, creeds and arguments. But it is the fundamental and common experience of religious peoples throughout the world and throughout history. Empowerment rather than argument is the common experience of the ages. Indeed scholars of religion, in contrast to theologians, point to example after example of the association of religion and power. In the Good Friday meditations we distinguished between fear of the known and fear of the unknown. At that time we observed that fear of the known is a very different kind of fear, namely dread. It is the experience of awe from which religious awareness arises. Scholars of religion have observed how this is frequently an experience of power. Not the power of the known. Not the power of a wild animal or an angry man. Not the power of the wind to blow down trees or the power of the river to wear through rock. Not the power of the known, but the power of the unknown. Not the power which is appropriate to the person or the thing, but a power which seems to have nothing to do with human or natural sources at all. It is an awesome power, unpredictible and uncontrollable. 'The wind blows where it wills, and you hear the sound of it, but you do not know whence it comes or whether it goes; so it is with every one who is born of the Spirit' (John 3.8). The Melanesians called it *mana*, the Iroquois called it *orenda*. To the Sioux Indians it was *wakanda*. In Borneo it was *petara*, while in Arabia it was *baraka*.[1] Always it is an experience of the Spirit which is not simply part of the human or natural world. It empowers men and women to do what they could not otherwise undertake.

When we enquire into the origins and nature of Christian faith, to seek the mystery *in* the events themselves, this is the point at which we begin, the empowerment of the disciples with the Spirit of God. Pentecost might seem a strange phenomenon in the modern world, but it is exactly what might be required as the starting point for a new faith which was to overpower the ancient world.

(*d*) *Life in the Spirit*

Fifty days after Passover the Jews celebrated the Feast of Weeks, coming at the end of the harvest. Its Greek name was *Pentecoste* and by the period we are considering it was associated with the giving of the law and the making of the Covenant at Sinai. Soon it would be associated with the giving of the Spirit and the making of a New Covenant. If the first covenant divided the Jews from the nations, this was to be a covenant to unite all nations.

> When the day of Pentecost had come, they were all together in one place. And suddenly a sound came from heaven like the rush of a mighty wind, and it filled all the house where they were

> sitting. And there appeared to them tongues as of fire, distributed and resting on each one of them. And they were all filled with the Holy Spirit, as the Spirit gave them utterance (Acts 2.1–4).

This was the kick-start required for the new movement, the church. *Mana, wakanda*: this was the Holy Spirit. Not of the human or natural world, it was a power which possessed the disciples and followers of Jesus. They were, in the words we have quoted from John's Gospel, 'born of the Spirit'. It was a great blessing, but not an unmixed blessing.

The church in Corinth seems to have been a particular trial at times to Paul. They had no lack of gifts of the Spirit, but this could also lead to division, as he points out in I Corinthians 12–14. Paul stressed the criterion that 'each is given the manifestation of the Spirit for the common good'. There is the spiritual gift of wisdom, of knowledge, of faith, of healing, of miracles and of prophesy. These were all used for the common good. The division was associated with the gift of speaking in tongues. This was clearly an exotic gift which many held in esteem. As such it could be a source of friction. It might be thought that Paul took a rather negative view of this phenomenon because he did not have the gift. Not so. 'I thank God that I speak in tongues more than you all . . . ' He applied his practical criterion. How does this gift benefit the life of the church? 'Let all things be done for edification.' In addition to the gift of tongues, there is the gift of interpretation of tongues. If an interpreter of tongues were present, then speaking in tongues could proceed. If not, then those with the gift of tongues should not exercise it in public. In this case the gift of prophesy was to be preferred. 'He who speaks in a tongue edifies himself, but he who prophesies edifies the church. Now I want you all to speak in tongues, but even more to prophesy.' From what Paul says there seem to have been two problems connected with speaking in tongues. The first was that it was regarded as an end in itself. As such it accorded status to the one who possessed the gift. He or she might be caught up in this exotic activity to the exclusion of more mundane acts. 'If I speak in the tongues of men and of angels, but have not love, I am a noisy gong or a clanging cymbal.' But Paul hints at a second problem. Quite apart from the fact that without interpretation speaking in tongues is a gift which edifies only the speaker and leaves the rest of the congregation out of account, it could have a very negative effect on unbelievers, possible converts who entered at that time: 'will they not say that you are mad?' It will be recalled that at Pentecost there was a special form of speaking in tongues. Some potential converts were intrigued by the phenomenon and enquired about its meaning and significance. Others thought they recognized such incoherence: 'they are filled with new wine.'

Pentecost therefore marks the birth of the church, since it was then that the disciples were reborn in the Spirit. Before that they were incapable of anything, thereafter they were capable of everything. At that time all their weaknesses were turned to strengths. In the first place these men who had lacked physical courage, who had denied Jesus and had gone into hiding, suddenly stood up in public and identified themselves as his followers. Since he had been condemned by the Jews for blasphemy they were indirectly associating with his alleged crime. That might have been a fine point, one which could have been argued. But as if to brush that aside Peter committed blasphemy on his own account. 'Let all the house of Israel therefore know assuredly that God has made him both Lord and Christ, this Jesus whom you crucified' (Acts 2.36). He proclaimed a crucified Messiah. More than that he directly accused those responsible for this deed.

Those who previously lacked courage were now fearless even when accusing the authorities. But secondly, those who lacked religious insight, indeed who were presented as lacking even common sense, now found the words with which to proclaim the new faith. With a mixture of scriptural texts and commentary thereon they preached Jesus as the risen Christ.

Thirdly, in fulfilment of the prophecy of John the Baptist, Peter called on his hearers to be baptized, not now simply with water, but with the Spirit. We are told that three thousand that day entered the church. Some might wonder about the physical possibility. Even beginning at the third hour, could three thousand people have been baptized in one day? For our purposes, however, the striking feature of the account is the authority which the apostles now assumed. Baptism is a strange action to perform on another person. It was not a common rite in Judaism, and as illustrated by John, it required compelling preaching and considerable personal authority to carry it off. Previously the disciples lacked such standing: now apparently they were entirely credible. They spoke not of themselves but in the Spirit.

There is a fourth element in this account. The church had its own liturgical life. Jesus had kept the Passover, and it may be that the apostles were in Jerusalem for Pentecost, the Festival of Weeks. But they discovered what Cleopas and his companion had experienced in Emmaus: 'he was known to them in the breaking of the bread' (Luke 24.35).

We noted earlier that although commissioned specifically to heal the sick, the disciples of Jesus were unable to perform such actions. But now, empowered by the Spirit, all that too was changed. 'And fear came upon every soul; and many wonders and signs were done through the apostles.' This is the same fear that we have already discussed, not fear of the threatening, of the known, but fear of the unknown. This is awe or dread. Those who were drawn into the early church did not simply enter an institution. The life in the Spirit was empowered by a presence not human or natural. Peter and John met a lame man begging at the temple gate. He asked alms, but was healed 'in the name of Jesus Christ of Nazareth'. What a curious title. As the Christ, now sitting at the right hand of the Father, he must be Lord of the universe. This he was to the disciples, and yet this was no faceless anonymous agent of God. Jesus Christ of Nazareth. Neither *mana* nor *wakanda*, but the Spirit. Not just spirit, but the Spirit of the same Jesus of Nazareth, present with enabling power in the lives of his disciples after his death. They recognized him now because they knew him then.

We can see the continuity between the historical Jesus and the Christ of the new faith. And we can see also the transformation in the disciples. That discontinuity is clear. Previously they could not search the scriptures, but now they can. They could not proclaim the good news, but now they can. They could not watch and pray, but now they can. They did not understand the Last Supper or his death, but now they do. They denied him and forsook him, but now they affirm him and call themselves by his name. This is the discontinuity yet continuity between the disciples and the apostles. Because they were close to Jesus in his life, their every word and action is regarded as having a peculiar authority for the church in succeeding ages. With one exception.

Guided by the Spirit the apostles made many decisions about the new faith, the new liturgy, the new community and its life together. All of these have been of intense interest to the church, except one.

> And all who believed were together and had all things in common; and they sold their possessions and goods and distributed them to all, as any had need (Acts 2.44–5).

What did the apostles teach on the subject of ministry, baptism, the Holy Spirit, the Trinity? None of these things is clear but that has not prevented groups in the church from taking up very precise positions on these matters and claiming apostolic authority for their views. By comparison it is quite clear what the apostles taught about the life of the community. They had experienced the communal life as disciples of Jesus. Now they reconstituted this communal life, except that with the bold initiative of those confident that they are led by the Spirit, they extended the community to include men and women. Strange to say this first authoritative and clear action taken by all the apostles acting together has never been regarded as having the slightest relevance to the life of the church. Nor has the church felt any obligation to take this apostolic institution as normative.

In our own day this has become a contentious matter. In America what is called the New Religious Right is perfectly clear that Christianity advocates capitalism. Representative of this view is Jerry Falwell, founder of the Moral Majority.

> The free-enterprise system is clearly outlined in the Book of Proverbs in the Bible. Ownership of property is biblical. Competition in business is biblical. Ambitious and successful business management is clearly outlined as a part of God's plan for His people.[2]

In contrast to this blatant religious legitimation of American capitalism its British counter-part is a more troubled association of the two, found in the writings of Brian Griffiths, economic adviser to Mrs Thatcher.

> I have always believed and continue to believe that the advocacy of monetarist policies is perfectly compatible with a Christian view of the world, and indeed that if such policies are seen as part of a general economic strategy to reduce the power of the state, give more power back to people, and to increase the

> participation of the individual family in economic life, then their basis is distinctly Christian.[3]

The first and decisive action of the apostles, what the church sociologist Ernst Troeltsch called 'the primitive communism of the Book of Acts',[4] is simply left out of account. In the ideological perspective of the Cold War it is simply assumed that communism is anti-Christian. Capitalism therefore must be Christian. By contrast the Mexican theologian and biblical scholar José Miranda claims, in his manifesto entitled *Communism in the Bible*, that for a Christian to claim to be anti-communist 'without doubt constitutes the greatest scandal of our century'.[5]

Pentecost marks the beginning of the Christian faith. We see at that moment the metamorphosis of the disciples into apostles, the reversal of all the features of their old lives and bad faiths portrayed in the Gospels, and the new life of empowerment in the Spirit. They were soon to be imprisoned and brought before the same Sanhedrin, and beaten. But they could not only face such things, they rejoiced that 'they were counted worthy to suffer dishonour for the name' (Acts 5.41). Soon the church would suffer its first martyrdom. Stephen was stoned to death, witnessing that the one who was judged now stands at the right hand of God. In confirmation of that terrible affirmation by Tertullian, 'The blood of Christians is seed',[6] Stephen's blood-stained robe was laid at the feet of a young Pharisee called Saul, thus planting the first seed of the faith that would spring up into a transformed Paul.

Pentecost was the foundation and the reality of Christian faith. The Spirit of Jesus Christ of Nazareth was alive powerfully in the lives of his disciples and followers. That was a matter of simple observation: even those who had killed Jesus recognized and feared as much. How this experience came to be linked to resurrection and an empty tomb is another matter and to this we must now turn.

8

The Appearances

(*a*) *Evidence of experience*

No one has ever been put in prison for dreaming dreams, for seeing visions or thinking thoughts. Only when these things begin to manifest themselves in ways which affect other people do they become a matter of public interest, and concern. As we have noted the church was born at Pentecost and without any decision or conscious intention found itself embodying the life of Jesus Christ of Nazareth. If the authorities had felt it necessary to take action against Jesus, they must have received the news with heavy sighs that, having cut down the plant, many shoots had reappeared. This is the foundation of Christian faith and life and it is not a matter of historical dispute: it was recognized by friend and foe alike. However, that is not how the origins of the church and Christian faith are normally presented. Instead they are linked to the resurrection of Jesus and to his appearance to his disciples and followers after his death. Thus resurrection has become a problem to Christians in the modern world, second only to the doctrine of the Trinity. Do we have to defend the resurrection before faith can begin? And how can we, some two thousand years removed, demonstrate the historicity of the appearances of Jesus to his disciples? Christians should never be put in such a position, and it is for this reason that we must examine closely the events, and distinguish them from theories and interpretations. The mystery after all is in the events, not the theories or explanations. If we understand them properly we shall find that we need have no anxieties about this matter. We shall not have to require of people in the modern world, including ourselves, any suspension of our best scientific or historical knowledge.

The first book which I wrote was concerned with Christian faith in modern, largely secular society.[1] I wanted to preserve the right balance. Yes, there were many things which should be criticized by Christian standards, but many things in which society knows better than those who lived in the ancient world. I aspired to being a Christian and a man of my own time and place. On the one hand I did not want to succumb to the assumptions of the age, on the other I did not want to be a Christian at the price of denying my own experience of life. I lived in the East Riding of Yorkshire and from time to time had occasion to go by train across the West Riding. On one such journey I happened to be reading the prison writings of Dietrich Bonhoeffer, from which I quoted earlier. At one point I looked out of the window at a landscape of industrial decay. There were rows of dark houses looking on to the sites of derelict factories. I looked back to the book and then out of the window again. It occurred to me that this was something of a test for theology: is it giving an account of things which is credible against such a landscape? Bonhoeffer, then in the hands of the Gestapo, passed the test. He maintained his faith in adverse circumstances; he preserved hope without illusions or delusions.

Christian faith requires – and deserves – that we be wise as serpents, as well as innocent as doves. There must be no special pleading for it, no suspension of our best knowledge of the world in which we live. Christian faith gives rise to hope, but our hope must not be founded on illusions or delusions. If we advocate religion to people on grounds that are suspect by modern standards then we offer them exactly what Marx claimed it to be, an opiate. Instead of disclosing reality, we disguise it from them. In shielding them from the pain we insulate them from the truth. Above all we must be utterly honest, honest with ourselves and with those we seek to influence. We should have no fear. Ultimately Christian faith cannot be defended or promoted through illusions. If it is true then we shall find a way to affirm it, even though it may not be on what have traditionally been assumed to be the grounds for its defence. What then are we to make of the assertion about the resurrection of Jesus? It is a sufficiently complex matter that we shall have to consider it in stages. We begin by considering the appearances of Jesus to his disciples and followers after his death.

Pentecost is the beginning of the Christian faith, the Christian church, the Christian life. It was at that point that the disciples and followers of Jesus were empowered. Not *mana*, not *wakanda*, but Spirit. Not Spirit in some general, phemonological sense, but that same Spirit which the disciples had experienced in the presence of Jesus. It was his Spirit then, and now it empowered their lives. Because of it they could now face danger and the threat of death. Now they could understand the deep things of God and now they were articulate to proclaim such mysteries. They, empowered by the Spirit of the ministry of Jesus were indeed and at last able to fulfil that commission laid upon them to heal the sick, raise the dead and preach good news to the poor. Not for a moment in their minds was there any doubt that this empowering spirit was the Spirit of Jesus, the Holy Spirit of God that had formerly empowered Jesus himself.

The conclusion was startling, but inescapable. Jesus was not dead, but alive. He was not consigned to hell, but affirmed in heaven. He the judged was now vindicated as judge, sitting at the right hand of God. 'Let all the house of Israel therefore know assuredly that God has made him both Lord and Christ, this Jesus whom you crucified.' This was the first proclamation of the new faith and it followed directly from the experience of the Spirit. Pentecost was the evidence for this conclusion. The corollory was that if the church does not live by power of the Spirit, then Christians have no evidence that Jesus lives. Not that everyone must be able to speak in tongues. As we have already seen, for Paul this was but one of the marks of the presence of the Spirit. The church, as the body of Christ, must corporately manifest the gifts of the Spirit, including wisdom, prophesy, healing, but above all love. Without the Spirit the credal beliefs have no substance and Christian faith is in vain. This was true of the first day of the life of the church and it is true even to our own day. We do not have evidence for or experience of events of that time. That is not our responsibility, but we do have the evidence and experience of the Spirit. With that we need no more: without it no amount of beliefs in exotic events will do.

The gifts of the Spirit were the original proof to the disciples and followers that Jesus lives, but not the first indications. Could they have moved to this conclusion directly? Could they have affirmed that Jesus lives if nothing had happened to them between the crucifixion and Pentecost? Who can say. Probably not. But in any case something did happen. Jesus appeared to them. It is quite clear there was no Christian faith before Pentecost, but the appearances of Jesus to his disciples and followers enabled them to receive the spirit as his Spirit, to see its effects as the empowerment to fulfil their calling. Put this way we can draw an important conclusion which will guide our meditations.

The appearances of Jesus to his first disciples and followers were necessary in order that at Pentecost Christian faith could arise. But it is possible to hold Christian faith without having experienced such an appearance. What the appearances actually were is therefore not of the substance of the Christian faith. It is not necessary for those who come later to feel that they must somehow affirm experiences which they have never had. Christians today hold their faith on the basis of their experience of their own new life in the Spirit of Christ. It is not a condition of holding that faith that they must somehow vouch for experiences which happened to other people remote in time and place. Without their testimony Christian faith would not have come down to us: but Christian faith having arisen in our lives it must be based on our experience, not theirs. The testimony is not now what they saw and heard and did, but what in turn we have seen, and heard and been enabled to do. And as before the corollory is that if we have no testimony of our own, repeating theirs is no substitute. 'If it is my will that he remain until I come, what is that to you? Follow me!' (John 21.22). We are not responsible for what they experienced, nor as historical record can we guarantee that it happened in any particular form. This may seem an abrasive position to adopt. The alternative would be disastrous, for it would require that before we could be Christian we should have to demonstrate the historical authenticity of events alluded to in fragments of Greek texts written almost two millenia ago. We might have opinions or beliefs about their interpretation, but that could never be the sufficient basis for a faith by which to live, and in extreme cases, for which to suffer and die.

In the light of this we can turn to the appearances with interest, but without anxiety. There is nothing at stake here. We do not have to argue with scientific determinism or historical relativism about whether and how such events could have happened. The important evidence is Pentecost and the transformation of the disciples brought about by that event. The appearances are not the basis of faith: they brought about no such empowerment. Indeed looked at more closely, it is never claimed that they added anything new not already known in the ministry of Jesus.

(*b*) *The Gospel appearances*

The first appearance in the Gospels was not to Peter or any of the disciples. It was to a follower, to a woman. The fact that we shall not consider it at this point is not because it is less important than other appearances, but on the contrary because it is so important that it will require to be examined separately.

Although the appearances of Jesus to his disciples after his death have been a subject of great interest and controversy, Matthew says very little indeed about the matter. In effect he simply reports that Jesus appeared to his disciples in Galilee. There is no indication of the time which had elapsed from the crucifixion, and we might reasonably expect that since the disciples had lost all faith and hope, they had returned to their homes. Jesus appeared to them there, on a mountain. The place would be one previously associated with him but it would now symbolize exaltation. Matthew adds a summary of the faith of the church which would have gradually emerged after Pentecost.

> All authority in heaven and on earth has been given to me. Go therefore and make disciples of all nations, baptizing them in the name of the Father and of the Son and of the Holy Spirit, teaching them to observe all that I have commanded you; and lo I am with you always, to the close of the age (Matt. 28.18–20).

The importance of the appearance is that it happened. No new teaching or information is conveyed beyond what had already been 'commanded' during his ministry. The revelation is *in* the event. The mere appearance is enough to raise the question whether after all the cross was the end, whether Jesus had been discredited, whether and how a new revelation of God was disclosed *in* the cross. Nothing new has to be said: something new has to be discerned.

Turning to Mark, scholars point out that the oldest Greek texts which we have end with the appearance to the women at the tomb. This may have been the end of the original Gospel, or it is possible that the final verses are missing for some reason. Further verses have been added by a later hand, though of course it is always possible that this addition only restored the original ending. However, in our new relaxed mode we are not prepared to become anxious about such considerations. It is all very interesting, not at all decisive for faith.

As we have the text now, Mark tells us that Jesus appeared to two of his disciples, or followers 'as they were walking into the country'. This could be taken to describe a Sunday afternoon nature ramble, but it is more likely that these travellers, like those going to Emmaus, were disillusioned men turning their backs on Jerusalem and returning home. One of the pseudo-scientific points made about the appearances in general is that they were the result of wish-fulfilment. As we saw earlier, however, all the wishes and hopes of the disciples were dashed at the cross. The new faith when it arose had nothing to do with what the disciples hoped for themselves. Indeed it in turn led them to suffering and in some cases to death. As if anticipating this objection Mark says that when the women told the disciples that Jesus had appeared to them 'they would not believe it'. Prejudice against women followers? No, because when the two travellers hurried back to recount their experience to the rest they did not believe them either. When Jesus subsequently appeared to the eleven together 'he upbraided them for their unbelief and hardness of heart'. The present ending of Mark, like that of Matthew, is an early statement of the faith of the church which would emerge only at Pentecost.

> Go into all the world and preach the Gospel to the whole creation. He who believes and is baptized will be saved; but he who does not believe will be condemned. And these signs will accompany those who believe: in my name they will cast out demons; they will speak in new tongues; they will pluck up serpents, and if they drink any deadly thing, it will not hurt them; they will lay their hands on the sick, and they will recover (Mark 16.15–18).

The addition describes the life of the empowered church after Pentecost. Nothing new is added by the appearance, but it raises the possibility of that reversal by which the judges are judged and the one who is vanquished is after all the victor.

It is in Luke's Gospel that we have the account of two of the followers of Jesus, not disciples, to whom Jesus appeared on the way to the village of Emmaus. They were leaving Jerusalem, turning their backs on the bad faith and dashed hopes, and did not recognize Jesus as he appeared to them. The situation is beautifully contrived. They patiently rehearse the events of the last few days to this 'stranger'. He in turn, unrecognized, shows them how to search the scriptures to discover the prophesies by which the events can be interpreted. This was in fact a technique which the church was to use extensively, after Pentecost. It is more likely that this appearance, like the others, included no long didactical exchange. That Jesus appeared to them was the substance, not a lesson in hermeneutics. This is confirmed when Luke tells us that Jesus did not appear to them as a teacher on the road, but 'in the breaking of the bread'.

The next appearance is linked to this one. The two return to report to 'the eleven', no doubt to be rejected out of hand, but Jesus suddenly appeared among them. Then follows another lesson in searching the scriptures. But Luke seems to acknowledge that nothing will begin until the empowerment. 'And behold, I send the promise of my Father upon you; but stay in the city, until you are clothed with power from on high' (Luke 24.49).

Finally we turn to John's Gospel. It too begins with the appearance to the women, which we shall consider later. Here also the testimony of the women is ignored. Even at this stage the disciples were hiding behind locked doors, 'for fear of the Jews'. Jesus appeared to them in the locked room. Once again the appearance is itself more important than any communication. There is added the by this time customary verses which reflect the experience of the church after Pentecost.

> 'Peace be with you. As the Father has sent me, even so I send you.' And when he had said this, he breathed on them, and said to them, 'Receive the Holy Spirit. If you forgive the sins of any, they are forgiven; if you retain the sins of any, they are retained' (John 20.21–2).

Mark's Gospel is full of incident with little of the teaching of Jesus. By contrast, in John's Gospel Jesus enters into long debates and discussions. So now in the appearance to the disciples by the Sea of Tiberias there is an extended interchange between Jesus and Peter, who is here called Simon. In it Jesus asks three times whether Peter loves him. Peter is grieved by this and it certainly echoes the three occasions in Luke when Peter denied Jesus. This is the same Peter, but things are soon to change. After Pentecost he will be empowered to affirm his allegiance to Jesus Christ, to be arrested, to obey God rather than men, to suffer and eventually to die for his new faith.

(*c*) *Incidence*

With the rise of critical thought in modern times the Gospel material on the appearances of Jesus has been the subject of debate. Indeed it has often been simply rejected out of hand rather than debated. The claim that Jesus appeared to his disciples after his death would seem unlikely, even absurd by any objective standards. By contrast are Christians, who also owe allegiance to the modern world of which they are members, to affirm the occurrence of supposed events which contradict contemporary knowledge and experience? In such matters are we suddenly to be as innocent and gullible as doves rather than as critical as wise serpents? What now of our call for honesty and avoidance of illusions? Three points should be made.

The first is that the tendency to reject possible events out of hand was typical of nineteenth-century thought, rather than twentieth-century. It was not so much scientific and objective thinking as ideology. To rule out certain things from happening arose from an attitude reflecting the scientific determinism of the day. Modern physics is anything but deterministic and is much more agnostic on what can and cannot happen. Linked to this was historical positivism, an equally confident view that the historian gave an account of the past, in von Ranke's words, *wie es eigentlich gewesen ist*, as it actually happened. Modern historical and literary studies make us less dogmatic about the treatment of ancient texts from cultures very different from our own.

The second point is that I have deliberately concentrated attention on the appearances of Jesus. These are described in the way that visions might be represented. With the increase in our knowledge of the complexities of the human psyche it is even less likely that such psychical events would be ruled out in an arbitrary manner. It will have been noted that as yet I have not dealt with those accounts of appearances which take on a definite physical character, for example when Jesus eats some broiled fish. We shall deal with these narratives later.

The third point concerns the frequency of the appearances. There is some suspicion about the appearances when they are reported to have been experienced by individuals, or small closed groups, especially in secret. So much has been made of the appearances, and yet in the first three Gospels there are very few indeed. Yet these were not the only appearances recorded in the early church.

We have already noted that Paul had trouble with the church in Corinth. It was a Greek city, but its Hellenistic culture had absorbed beliefs, customs and values from many traditions. Indigenization has become something of a slogan in modern missionary situations. Paul had already experienced that, and was concerned that in expressing their new faith in terms of Hellenistic culture the Corinthians might lose contact with the historical roots of Christian faith. In I Corinthians 15 Paul therefore reminds them not simply of his own understanding but of the tradition which was passed on to him from the first generation of the church, many of whom had known Jesus and had participated in the historic events.

> For I delivered to you as of first important what I also received, that Christ died for our sins in accordance with the scriptures, that he was buried, that he was raised on the third day in accordance with the scriptures, and that he appeared to Cephas, then to the twelve.

Here it would seem is a unique event, the appearance of Jesus to Peter, and to the other disciples. (To the twelve, not the eleven. Does this refer to the period after the ascension, when Matthias was chosen to replace Judas? Or is it a simple mistake?) How can the Corinthians be expected to found their faith on such secondary testimony? Did the appearance to the disciples happen, just as reported? In fact the issue is not as important as it at first sight appears. 'Then he appeared to more than five hundred brethren at one time, most of whom are still alive, though some have fallen asleep.' This must be a reference to the church after Pentecost. It is impossible to imagine a gathering of five hundred of the disciples and followers of Jesus taking place after the crucifixion, like some class reunion. It could only be a gathering of members of the new church. But with this the whole matter is completely transformed. We serpents might be rightly suspicious if we heard of an extraordinary event which had taken place in private before a small band of committed individuals. But if the same event occurs before some five hundred individuals, many of whom are still available to be questioned about it, then the whole basis of the enquiry is changed. There is no longer any point to denying that such appearances occurred. We must rather enquire into their nature and significance. In other words, far from being something very exclusive and private, the appearances would seem to be not at all uncommon in the life of the early church.

(*d*) *The due time*

In the Gospels it seems that the appearances were restricted in several ways. They were experienced only by the close friends of Jesus. For the most part they occurred in places specifically associated with him. But from what Paul reports they were now being experienced by people who had no association with Jesus during his ministry. And of course in the conversion experience of Saul himself on the road to Damascus Jesus was addressing someone who did not know him during his ministry, in a place with which he was not associated. Whether strictly this was counted as an appearance of Jesus or not is not clear, but Paul asserts that he too has experienced an appearance. 'Then he appeared to James, then to all the apostles. Last of all, as to one untimely born, he appeared also to me.'

The reference presumably is to his rebirth as a Christian. By that time the appearances of Jesus to his first disciples and followers, and then to the new converts to the church, had become less frequent. Anyone who entered the church in the first days or weeks would not have been surprised to experience the appearance of Jesus. As time passed they became less frequent, till by the time Paul was converted it was unusual.

What then is the relationship between the appearances and Christian faith? The appearances were not the foundation of the faith. That was the empowerment at Pentecost. The appearances enabled the disciples to identify the Holy Spirit of Pentecost with the spirit of Jesus, to affirm that reversal which runs throughout the life of Jesus. But having an appearance was not a condition of being a Christian. The evidence was in the empowerment, not the historical reports. The answer is in the risen Christ's words to Thomas in John's Gospel: 'Have you believed because you have seen me? Blessed are those who have not seen and yet believe.' The appearances without the Spirit signify nothing: with the coming of the Spirit the appearances no longer served any purpose.

9

The Empty Tomb

(*a*) *Dreams and visions*

Many of the things which attract our attention in the Bible would not seem unusual in the ancient world. No one denied that Jesus was able to perform miracles. Miracle workers, it would seem, were not uncommon in those days: attention focussed rather on the source of the miraculous powers. Were they of God or Satan? We have noted the reference to the dream of Pilate's wife. Robin Lane Fox in his exhaustive, or at least exhausting, study of *Pagans and Christians* makes it clear that this was a trusted means of communication between the divine and human spheres. 'In their dreams, pagans of all classes and backgrounds kept the closest company with gods.'[1] It would not seem at all odd for pagans to hear from Matthew's Gospel that an angel of the Lord appeared to Joseph in a dream to warn him of the danger to the child. In his sermon at Pentecost Peter refers to such phenomena, by adapting a prophesy of Joel.

> And in the last days it shall be, God declares,
> that I will pour out my Spirit upon all flesh,
> and your sons and your daughters shall prophesy,
> and your young men shall see visions
> and your old men shall dream dreams (Acts 2.17;cf.Joel 2.28).

For Jesus to appear to his followers in dreams and visions was what might be expected in a community of the Spirit in the ancient world. As Fox notes, 'That God could visit man was the least novel feature of Christian teaching in a pagan's eyes.'[2]

That Jesus appeared to his disciples and followers after his death would prove nothing to those who first heard the proclamation of the early church. The visions were sufficiently frequent that it would seem today but ideological dogmatism to deny that they took place, but more importantly it is not claimed that they demonstrated anything in themselves. We are not being asked to accept anything solely on the strength of the assertion about appearances. The evidence, ancient and modern, for the Christian faith lies in the empowerment, an objective, demonstrable occurrence.

As long as we restrict the appearances of Jesus to the sphere of visions and dreams apparently there are no real grounds for objection. But for some reason that was not good enough for the Gospel writers. Earlier we noted that there are other appearances, or other aspects of the appearances which go well beyond visions. In these cases the appearances include physical, material elements. To these we must now turn our attention.

(*b*) *Materialization*

Of the appearances we have already discussed in Matthew and Mark, none is extended in a material direction. By contrast in Luke the appearance to the two on the road to Emmaus would seem to be more material. We previously noted that the original extent of the appearance was probably in Emmaus, in the house, rather than in an extended lecture on biblical interpretation on the dusty road. But in the house the appearance takes a material form: 'When he was at table with them, he took the bread and blessed, and broke it, and gave it to them. And their eyes were opened and they recognized him; and he vanished out of their sight' (Luke 24.30–11). Clearly this is not simply a vision of Jesus, nor for that matter is it simply Jesus alive again as he was before death. There is a flickering ambiguity: he materializes to them on the way, and when they recognize him he dematerializes – as if somehow when they get the message that he is alive there is no further need of appearance.

Following on from that there is a more specific materialization. Jesus appeared to the disciples, and chided them when they acted as though they had seen a ghost! 'Why are you troubled, and why do questionings arise in your hearts? See my hands and my feet, that it is I myself; handle me and see; for a spirit has not flesh and bones as you see that I have' (Luke 24.38–9). Here are the terrible wounds inflicted by the nails and the hours of suspension on the cross. And if all this could still be some ghostly vision Jesus proves his identity to them by one of the two most normal of human actions. He calls for bread and wine? No, he has already done that and they did not believe it. ' "Have you anything here to eat?" They gave him a piece of broiled fish, and he took it and ate before them.' What could be more reassuring to fishermen than that he should eat some fish?

However, it is in John's Gospel that the appearances of Jesus are extended farthest in a material direction. It is of profound significance that it is in this work, often regarded as the most spiritual of Gospels, that the risen Christ takes on the most material of forms. There is the same ambiguity that we have already noted in Luke. Jesus comes to his disciples 'the doors being shut', but he shows them his hands and also the wound in his side. This is enough to convince everyone who was in the room, but Thomas was not with them. Thomas is not singled out in the other three Gospels but in John's Gospel he makes the comment that we have earlier discussed as they go to the raising of Lazarus. Later his confusion about where Jesus is going provides the occasion of the great saying: 'I am the way, the truth and the life . . . ' (John 14.6). Now once again he is remembered not for his insight or understanding, but because he says honestly what anyone else would say in such a situation: 'Unless I see in his hands the print of the nails, and place my finger in the mark of the nails and place my hand in his side, I will not believe' (John 20.25). A week later Jesus appears again, the doors being shut, and offers him precisely this test. Which Thomas then declines. The writer claims that all these constitute but a selection of the many signs: 'but these are written that you may believe that Jesus is the Christ, the Son of God, and that believing you may have life in his name' (John 20.31).

This would be an appropriate point at which to end the Gospel, but there now follow two further, detailed, appearance accounts, the first of which is highly materialized. The occasion is a fishing trip undertaken on the Sea of Tiberias by Peter, Thomas, Nathaniel, James and John, and two other disciples who for some reason are not named. Naturally attention has focussed on Jesus appearing to them, but we might pause to consider the circumstances. We have been maintaining that Christian faith and belief begin with Pentecost and the empowerment. Before that the appearances raise questions but settle nothing. As we have frequently observed, there is a tendency for the evangelists to write their faith back into the time when the disciples were with Jesus. There is good historical evidence to suggest that there was no Christian faith before the cross and resurrection. The accounts of the appearances similarly suggest that there was Christian faith and belief before Pentecost, but that too is unlikely. Support for this comes at this very point in John's Gospel. Chapter 20 involves the confession of faith of Thomas, who now believes, the comforting words addressed to those of us who come later – 'Blessed be those who have not seen and yet believe' – and the concluding verses indicating that these selections are provided so that we who read might believe and have life. Chapter 20 ends, therefore, with the risen Christ, the believing church and the message to the world. Chapter 21 begins with some of the disciples deciding to go on a fishing trip. Clearly the appearances did not launch faith, belief and world mission. There was something of a hiatus. Questions were raised, but nothing was clarified till Pentecost. Then indeed did faith, belief and mission arise with all the full-time commitment and energy of an empowered community.

The incident at the Sea of Tiberias is typical of the theological style of the writer of the Fourth Gospel. Throughout the ministry of Jesus there are events and meetings heavily imbued with a sense of the supernatural. Jesus is surrounded by mystery, to the confusion of the men and women who encounter him. So here there is the fruitless night in the boat, but as the darkness gives way to the new dawn, Jesus appears and directs them to a catch of fish. Typically it is too great for them, yet just as mysteriously the net does not tear. We are not told that Jesus set a fire, but fire there is and breakfast is cooked. He provides them with bread and with fish, but not the fish they have caught. It is a materialized appearance, but very much in the theological mode of this Gospel.

What then are we to make of these materialized appearances? They are certainly ambiguous, in two respects. The first is that there is a flickering as we have noted between the material and the non-material. The risen Jesus materializes to his disciples, but the doors are shut. The second is that the appearances have become very detailed with respect to faith and belief, and yet they do not of themselves effect any change. That is to say the material appearances do not achieve anything more than the visionary appearances.

The question therefore is not what do the materialized appearances achieve, but why are there such appearances at all? Or rather why are some appearances described as if they had been material? The answer in a word is Docetism. In the Good Friday meditation we referred to Docetism frequently. Then we made two points about it. The first point was that Docetism was the earliest heresy to appear within the church. The second point was that it was never defeated and it is well represented in the church to this day. Now in the Easter meditation we shall find that these two points must be reiterated.

As the earliest heresy to appear within the church Docetism arose with respect to the belief in the resurrection. Only later did it extend its interpretation of events back into the life and ministry of Jesus. We have examined this development and the attempts of the evangelists to combat it, but it first emerged in the context of Easter. In dealing with the earlier material we observed that Docetism seemed extreme and less than credible: Jesus not really human, some one else substituted for him to die on the cross. But these were but the outworking of its basic premise. It might be weak and less attractive in these ramifications, but apparently it was particularly attractive in its central position.

For Docetism things are not as they seem: the divine does not merge with the human, neither does the spiritual with the material. The appearances of Jesus were therefore exactly what Docetists would expect. For them Jesus did not die a human death and he was soon present again to his disciples and followers. On their view he had never been material and therefore had easily escaped the cross. On their assumptions the difficulty was to see how Jesus could apparently have lived an ordinary human life: this involved pretence and disguise. But now they were on stronger grounds. Liberated at last from the body, the material, the human, their Jesus appeared as he really was, a divine being. He could of course appear and disappear at will. He could move instantly from one place to another, and could enter a room the doors being shut. Docetism was perfectly receptive to the Spirit moving at will without restriction.

The farther Docetism went the stronger it became. It was least credible in dealing with the human life of Jesus. It was much more at ease with the visionary appearances after death. And it was entirely open to empowerment by the Holy Spirit. But if Docetism had become the dominant tradition within the church then it would have destroyed the true historical basis of Christian faith. In our terms it would have been the negation and rejection of the revelation *in* the events. No new self-manifestation of God would have been allowed to appear.

The church was therefore in considerable difficulty. The appearances of Jesus were central to the continuity between the revelation and the new life in Christ. Yet the appearances were susceptible to a Docetic interpretation. Earlier we said that in order to flush Docetism out into the open it was necessary to ask whether Jesus actually suffered, whether he died a human death. Docetism could not accept such events. Similarly Docetism could not accept that the risen Jesus was the one who had actually suffered and died. For the Docetists it was inconceivable that Jesus could appear with actual wounds in his hands and side. In other words they could not envisage any material form of appearance which acknowledged that the human life and death of Jesus had been really that.

For this reason the appearances of the risen Jesus were subject to a process of materialization in the early church. Here he takes a loaf of bread and breaks it, there he eats some broiled fish. Now he offers his hands and his side for their inspection, later prepares breakfast by the sea shore. The effect was to close the door to Docetism, a necessary and important goal, but it was achieved at some cost. It solved one problem, but spawned more in its wake. These problems have exercised subsequent generations of Christians, but they also caused difficulties even for some of the writers in the New Testament.

(*c*) *A tradition develops*

I recall my New Testament teacher, Professor John Knox, saying that whenever a question was raised in the early church concerning the status of Jesus, they always chose the higher alternative. When the disciples and followers began to reflect on the implications of the fact that Jesus was alive they first of all concluded that because of his death he was made Christ. But having said that they were faced with another question. If he was declared Christ at his resurrection had he not been designated Christ during his life? And that in turn led back to the conclusion that if he was designated Christ during his life, he must have been chosen at the moment of conception. There is something of a parallel in the subject now before us. The original appearances were visionary: Jesus appeared among them suddenly. He did not make his way towards them. The doors were shut. Having appeared to Cleopas and his companion, he simply vanished, he did not leave the room. But that, as we have seen, opened the door to Docetism, to the view that Jesus had never been truly human and material at any time. In order to answer the Docetists the church presented the appearances as in part material. See the mark of the nails, the wound in the side. This is the same Jesus who suffered and died. But if these marks were material, so that Thomas could have touched them, then the risen Jesus must have been part of the material world. He could be known in the breaking of bread. And if it was the same Jesus who was human, then he might enjoy a little broiled fish.

We are inclined to think that fixed positions were immediately reached in the early church, but a moment's thought suggests that their insight into situations would be progressive. If Jesus had to 'increase in wisdom', this would be true also for the first Christians as for Christians of every age. In order to close the door to Docetism the church was committed to a progressive materialization of the appearances of Jesus. Each position adopted turned out to be only provisional: each raised questions which pressed the writers farther along a particular path. And at the end of that path there could be but one end point: the empty tomb. Eventually the materialization of the appearances led to a final question. If the risen Jesus was so material that his disciples could be invited to touch the wounds, that he could break a loaf of bread, that he could eat some fish, then surely his tomb must be empty.

(*d*) *The empty tomb*

Many Christians today find the empty tomb a considerable problem, and rightly so. In fact there are two very different problems raised by the tradition of the empty tomb. The first concerns what happened. When I was a student I first heard of a book by Frank Morrison with the intriguing title *Who Moved the Stone?* But even at that time it suggested to me an alternative question. Why was it necessary to move the stone at all? The ambiguity of the question, who moved the stone, is an instance of that flickering ambiguity to which we have already referred. It is never said of the risen Jesus that he made his way from place to place: he simply appeared and vanished. This is the Jesus of the visionary appearances, what I take to be the earlier form. Clearly as the process of materialization continued the logic was that the tomb must be empty. If Jesus was present in such material form then this must be his actual body, and the tomb must be empty. And if the material body rose from the dead then the stone would have to be rolled away to allow Jesus to leave the tomb. Without any intention to shock religious sensibilities I must say that I find this crass materialism highly distasteful. It certainly closes the door to Docetism, but the price is too high. There must be another and better way.

You will notice that because of the direction of approach I am entirely relaxed about the whole issue. It causes me no anxiety at all. The reason will be clear. The starting point for Christian faith is not the discovery of an empty tomb, but the empowerment by the Spirit. The starting point for Christian faith is not the appearances of Jesus to his disciples and first followers. We who have not seen, who came too late, are in no way disadvantaged. And now it is but a further step to say that the basis of Christian faith is the baptism of the Spirit of Jesus, and the crass materialism of an empty tomb has nothing at all to do with this experience. Why the tradition of the empty tomb has become a problem and a cause of concern to many Christians today is because they have been led to believe – quite falsely – that Christian faith depends on it: if the tomb is not empty your faith is in vain. Be assured: this is not the case. The empty tomb is not the basis of anything, and certainly not Christian faith. The problem and confusion arises when the empty tomb is taken to be the starting point. It is assumed that this is the first fact, and it must be established or accepted, before we can move any farther.

It will be clear that we have taken a very different route. We have not begun with the empty tomb, but ended with it. We have not made it the starting point, but a distant end point: not the premise of faith, but the unfortunate consequence of the struggle with a particular heresy. For this reason we know how the tradition has come about. We can understand it, without accepting it. It has nothing to do with Christian faith, faith that Jesus Christ of Nazareth has conquered death and now stands at the right hand of God. We must not allow ourselves to be pushed into a false position, as if to be indifferent to the tradition of the empty tomb was to be uncertain about the new life in Christ. There is no necessary connection between the two. Another of my former teachers, Ronald Gregor Smith, once wrote that the bones of Jesus lie somewhere in Palestine.[3] You can imagine the shock this caused, and the abusive, dismissive response it elicited. But if we begin with the Spirit, if we understand the empty tomb as an unfortunate consequence of the route taken in answering Docetism, then we can agree with Gregor Smith. Indeed we can go farther. For if the body of Jesus did not go down to dust, then his life was not human after all, and he did not die as we all die. The tradition of the empty tomb, far from closing the door to Docetism, hands it the final victory by a different route.

Earlier I said that the empty tomb raised two very different problems for Christians today. The first was to know what happened. This we have addressed. The second is an issue on which we have already touched. The empty tomb is a matter of historical fact. Either it was empty or it was not. The way in which historical questions are answered is through a critical consideration of the best historical data available. In this case the data is meagre indeed. And if we could answer the question in the affirmative, that when the women returned to the tomb it was indeed empty, what conclusion would follow from that? It is notoriously difficult to draw a positive conclusion from a negative situation. Throughout history, and also in the present, ordinary men and women have faced suffering and death rather than deny the Lord whose Spirit empowers them. They can testify that Jesus Christ of Nazareth lives in them and they in him. If necessary they can give up life rather than deny the true source of life within them. But who could face suffering and death to affirm fragmentary reports from two thousand years ago that a tomb was empty? Faith has its own knowledge, but on purely historical matters it has no data beyond what is publicly available. The empty tomb was never the starting point for faith, never the basic evidence or experience which gave rise to faith. We need feel no anxiety about it: it is no indicator of being a Christian or not.

But how can this be? Is the affirmation of the empty tomb not part of the Christian *credo*? The answer of course is No. It is not part of the creeds of the church. The faith is that Jesus Christ of Nazareth, having suffered death, now lives and reigns in heaven. This is the faith that begins with Pentecost and the tradition of the empty tomb has no part in it. But is it not at least implied? No, not even that. Indeed if we pursue this line of enquiry something very significant emerges. You may have noted that I have taken to using the phrase 'the tradition of the empty tomb'. Even if the empty tomb was not a historical event, there is a tradition about an empty tomb, and this tradition has its own history. In order to make this distinction it would be as well if we could indicate the circumstances and the period when the tradition first appeared. As to the circumstances, we have argued that it arose in a period when the church was combatting Docetism. It is prominent in the Gospels and they are normally regarded as having been written in the last quarter of the first-century. The tradition of the empty tomb was widely known therefore by the end of the century. But what of earlier Christian writers? We could of course choose some obscure authors who wrote very little, but there would equally be little to be gained from this. We should go instead to Paul himself.

We have already quoted from I Corinthians 15, that great passage in which Paul deals with the resurrection. Some of the Christians in that city had strayed from Paul's teaching on the subject and he wrote to recall them to the mainstream. Indeed he went farther than that. Instead of guiding them on his own authority, he cited to them the tradition. 'For I delivered to you as of first importance what I also received . . . ' We have already reviewed that passage. In recalling the Corinthians to the true faith, the faith of the tradition, he brings before them an impressive list of witnesses. Christ is risen. He appeared to Cephas, and then to the twelve. He appeared to over five hundred, and if the Corinthians cared to do so it would still be possible to speak to some of that number. What more can Paul say to convince them? Well, the risen Christ appeared also to James (perhaps he was known to some of the Corinthians), and to all the apostles. Having brought forward every piece of evidence which he could from the tradition Paul finally adds his own testimony. The risen Christ appeared to the apostles, and even to that lately come apostle, that apostle born out of season, Paul himself. And there Paul must rest his case. If they are not persuaded on this weight of testimony, what more can be said?

In this review of the tradition Paul gives us information which is not found anywhere else in the New Testament. He was clearly familiar with the tradition of the earliest days of the church: he tells us elsewhere that he made it his business to do just that. It is therefore all the more striking that he does not mention the empty tomb. He has brought forward every piece of testimony available to him, but this he does not include. The obvious conclusion is that he knew nothing of it. Docetism was not yet an issue for the church and therefore the process which we have described as the materialization of the appearances had not yet begun.

What conclusion should we draw from all of this? The evidence points us towards the fact that the tradition of the empty tomb was late: it arose from a struggle with heresy, rather from historical events. The mystery is not *in* the empty tomb: it was not an event. But if these matters still seem ambiguous, then one conclusion is perfectly clear. For Paul, for the early church – and for us today – it was possible to affirm the Christian faith without reference to an empty tomb.

10

The Companion of Jesus

(*a*) *The first witness*

It will now be clear why we could not begin this Easter meditation simply by going to the empty tomb to observe the women on the first day of the week, after the sabbath. Christian faith does not begin with the empty tomb: we had to begin elsewhere. And what a relief that is. Now we need not consider this episode in the Gospels as if everything depended upon it. We have seen the value of the tradition of the empty tomb for the mission of the church, and problems associated with it. Now we must examine the *tradition* of the women who first went to the tomb. We are not now concerned with physico-historical questions of whether and how such a thing could happen. Instead we ask what this tradition tells us about Christian faith.

We have just concluded that Paul knew nothing of a tradition about an empty tomb, but he not only knew of appearances – many and frequent appearances – but had himself experienced an appearance of Jesus. Traditions grow, develop and become detailed and complex, but they normally arise from some historical basis. In the case of the tradition of the empty tomb we can assume that the tradition goes back to the women who did indeed go to the tomb, and there experienced an appearance, the first appearance of Jesus. From that non-contentious starting point the complex tradition developed in the light of circumstances which threatened the faith towards the end of the century.

Good Friday ended with Mary Magdalene and the other Mary, the mother of James and Joseph, sitting across from the tomb as Joseph of Arimathea departed. According to the tradition in Matthew they returned, as soon as the sabbath observance permitted. They were still in the same condition as they had been on the Friday: without faith or hope. They went to the tomb not in quiet confidence or with any expectations at all, but with heavy hearts to perform one last rite on the body of Jesus. Instead they were confronted at the tomb by the appearance of Jesus. In view of the frequency of such appearances over the next few weeks there is no reason to doubt its authenticity. But around that historical event there later accumulated a more and more complex tradition of materialization, required to defeat Docetism. The appearance then took on more substantial form. They were able to take hold of his feet in a gesture of submission and worship. Such a material Jesus must have required the stone to be rolled away from the tomb. Who moved the stone? An angel of the lord came directly from heaven to do it. Alternatively this later tradition tells of an earthquake which displaced the great stone. The angel made the announcement of the resurrection and the women became the first of many hundreds of thousands to be given a brief tour of the sepulchre.

Mark as usual has a more detailed narrative. As we have previously mentioned, scholars believe that the original ending of the Gospel has been lost. This assumption, that Mark should have said much the same as the others, was shared by the early church, and four brief notes have been added. As it stands Mark has the discovery of the empty tomb, but no appearance. To that is added a verse indicating that the first appearance was to Mary Magdalene. Then there is a parallel to the Lukan incident at Emmaus. This is followed by the appearance of Jesus to the disciples, and the commission to preach the new faith throughout the world. There is finally, in contrast to the other Gospels, a reference to the ascension.

Mark notes that the women went to the tomb carrying the materials they would need, but they were not sure how they would be able to perform these last rites, since they were unlikely to receive any help in that place so early in the day. They need not have worried; the stone was already moved. On seeing and being addressed by an angel within, they fled trembling and astonished. According to Mark they told no one of this experience. Since this is not only different from what might be expected, but from what the other Gospels say, we must assume that this is indeed how Mark from his own specific and particular perspective intended his Gospel to end: faith did not follow the empty tomb.

Luke tells of the women going with spices to the tomb. The

stone had been rolled away, and when they entered the tomb it was empty. They were addressed by two angels concerning the significance of all this, and then they went off to tell the disciples. But although the report came from Mary Magdalene, Joanna and Mary the mother of James the disciples did not believe a word of it. No appearance of Jesus to the women is mentioned. In this Mark and Luke are agreed. On the road to Emmaus Cleopas and his companion described how some of them went to investigate the women's account, and although they found the tomb empty, they saw nothing else.

There are similarities between Luke's form of the tradition and that given in John's Gospel. Here only Mary Magdalene is reported as going to the tomb, though later when speaking to Peter the implication is that she was accompanied. She discovered the empty tomb: nothing more. On telling this to the disciples, two of them rushed to the scene. They saw that the tomb was empty apart from the grave clothes, but nothing else. Once again the woman is represented as the sensible one. The beloved disciple saw the empty tomb 'and believed'. But what would you believe if you saw an empty tomb? Mary drew the more obvious, common sense conclusion. 'They have taken the Lord out of the tomb, and we do not know where they have laid him' (John 19.2).

To digress briefly, we might reflect that if we were merely dealing with the mystery of an empty tomb, then the most obvious solution is that proposed by Mary. If the tomb was empty, then someone had removed the body. The disciples of Jesus were beyond suspicion. They were hiding for fear of the authorities and would not identify themselves by associating with Jesus' body in any way. Nor would the followers of Jesus have taken the body. The women went to the tomb expecting the body of Jesus to be there. The Jewish authorities in turn were beyond suspicion, since if they had taken the body this would have been the basis of their attack upon the new sect and its proclamation that Jesus rose from the dead. If we were simply dealing with an empty tomb, then the prime suspects would be the Romans. One of the features of that volatile mixture of religion and nationalism is the commemoration of martyrs, and annual association at the grave of the fallen hero. Although the centurion might have released the body from the cross to Joseph of Arimathea, for a consideration, that may well have been against imperial policy. When the Roman authorities discovered this they could have removed the body, to forestall any future associations. All that, if we were simply dealing with an empty tomb. 'They have taken the Lord out of the tomb, and we do not know where they have laid him' (John 19.2). However, we are not dealing simply with an empty tomb, but with a much more complex tradition.

Earlier we discussed the encounter with Jesus which the two travellers had on their way to Emmaus. The incident is beautifully recounted. We know that they are speaking to Jesus, but they do not. They are sorrowful, but if they only recognized him they would be joyful. But they did not. Worse, they went on recounting to him the events of the last few days, events involving Jesus himself. Without irreverence it is like a scene in the theatre when the children in the audience can see what the players apparently cannot. 'Look out!' 'He's coming!' While reading Luke's account we want to say, 'It's him!' In John's Gospel there now follows a similar scene. When Mary discovered the empty tomb she drew the obvious conclusion: the body had been removed. She followed the two disciples back to the tomb, and when they had gone away again, having seen nothing, she stayed on. Have you ever been in the situation, perhaps at a railway station, when the people you have come to meet have not turned up. Trains come and go. There is no point in staying on, but going away makes less sense. So Mary stayed on, although nothing was happening. Or again, have you ever looked for something in the place where you know it should be, perhaps in a box, and it is not there? You are confused and fitfully look in a few other places where you know it certainly cannot be. And then you look again in the box, where you now know it is not. The narrative is beautifully told. Mary went back to the tomb, and after a while looked in again. Was she expecting the body to be there after all? Still no body of Jesus, just two angels. What more natural than that they should ask why she is crying. They know, and we know, but Mary does not know. She, poor woman, is still stunned by the gross deed, that the body should have been taken unceremoniously away by uncaring hands. 'Because they have taken away my Lord, and I do not know where they have laid him' (John 20.13). 'They' have done it, as 'they' always do, without reason or consideration. 'They' never have the grace or humanity to treat anything as sacred if it belongs to the weak or the poor.

But now the writer heightens the emotional level once again. Mary turns and is confronted by Jesus – but she does not recognize him. 'It's him!' 'It's him!' In this Gospel we are given more details about the burial. The site, not far from Golgotha was not a barren place, but a garden, and Mary assumed that she was being questioned about her behaviour or even her presence there by someone who had a right to be there, perhaps the gardener. If he is one of them, then she must show some respect if she is to find out what happened. 'Sir, if you have carried him away, tell me where you have laid him, and I will take him away.' 'It's him!' But she cannot see it. They recognized him in the breaking of bread. She recognized him when he spoke her name. Not Mary, but the more intimate 'Mariam'. She responded, not Master, but 'My Master'.

(*b*) *The first apostle*

As we saw earlier the disciples were completely transformed at Pentecost. Previously they had been presented to us as of less than average common sense and religious insight. From that time on they became leaders of great moral courage and religious initiative. But the empty tomb came before Pentecost, and in this tradition the earlier pattern continued. On the first day of the week, the first available opportunity, the women rose early, long before dawn, to fulfil their last obligations. The disciples by comparison were still fearfully hiding away. It was to the women that Jesus first appeared, not to the disciples. They had remained with him to the end, and it was fitting that they should be the first to see him. But when they sought to share their joy with the disciples, the men did not believe them. At least in Matthew and Luke they did not believe them. In John it was even worse: the beloved disciple believed an empty tomb. As before the death of Jesus, so after, the women followers displayed fidelity and common sense.

Given this situation a stranger, unacquainted with the development of the Christian church, might be forgiven for supposing that it would be a movement led by women. Jesus chose male disciples; his female followers chose him. But in the appearances the order was reversed. Jesus chose to appear first not to his disciples, but to his women followers. Nor was this simply a matter of being at the right place at the right time, being first at the tomb. Being first at the tomb had its own significance, but that was not decisive. In

John's Gospel Peter went to the garden and rushed right into the tomb. Since they had not been there at the burial, presumably he was dependent on Mary Magdalene to point it out to him. But apart from the grave clothes, he saw nothing. It was after his departure that Mary was confronted first by two angels and then by Jesus himself. In other words, according to this version of the tradition Jesus deliberately concealed himself from Peter, in order that Mary should be the first witness of the resurrection.

On this account Mary was given preference over Peter. Jesus chose the one who had chosen him, rather than the one whom he had chosen. The revelation was given first to a woman. This is the Gospel of John, but not of Paul.

> As in all the churches of the saints, the women should keep silence in the churches. For they are not permitted to speak, but should be subordinate, as even the law says. If there is anything they desire to know, let them ask their husbands at home. For it is shameful for a woman to speak in church. What! Did the word of God originate with you, or are you the only ones it has reached? (I Cor. 14.33–36).

Of all the things this Pharisee brought with him into the new Christian community, one was the inferior place of women – 'as even the law says'. This inferiorization of women is not to be sought in some minor work of the Hebrew scriptures, but in the law of Moses, not in some obscure corner of the canon, but right there the opening chapters of Genesis. The Garden of Eden was made for man, and woman too was made for man. Man was given responsibility for the garden, woman was created to be his 'helper'. As a punishment for disobedience man was put out of the garden. But part of woman's punishment was to be subordinate to man: 'and he shall rule over you' (Gen. 3.16). As a male Jew Paul was justified in saying that women should be under the control of men, 'as even the law says'. However, he was not justified in saying it as a Christian. 'What! Did the word of God originate with you . . . ?' Yes, according to the Gospel of John.

Indeed this tradition that Jesus preferred Mary to Peter continued in Christian communities into the second and third centuries. We know this from extensive collections of Christian writings of that period, which were excluded from the New Testament. These documents preserved old traditions in the church, even if their theology diverged from the emerging orthodoxy. They were non-canonical, excluded from the canon of the New Testament, but not without historical value. In John's Gospel Mary was sent to proclaim the risen and ascended Jesus to the disciples. For this reason Mary Magdalene, or Mariam, was to be known in the early church as 'the apostle of the apostles'.[1] In one of these non-canonical documents to which we have referred she was addressed by the risen Lord as 'sister' and was commonly referred to as the 'companion' of Jesus. Of her special religious insight and wisdom there was no question. 'This word she spoke as a woman who knew the All.'[2] In the same source her unique status as apostle to the apostles affirmed. 'Because you reveal the greatness of the revealer.'[3] In another source it is she who keeps up a flood of questions to Jesus, till Peter complains, 'My Lord, let the woman cease to question, that we also may question.'[4]

In these ancient documents Mariam's special relationship to Jesus is generally acknowledged, even among the other apostles. 'Peter said to Mary, "Sister, we know that the Saviour loved you more than the rest of women . . . " '[5] Peter asked that Mary should reveal to them the secret teachings which Jesus had given to her alone. But even if she had a special place among women, neither Andrew nor Peter could accept her authority. 'Did he really speak privately to a woman and not openly to us? Are we to turn about and all listen to her? Did he prefer her to us?'[6] But in this the ancient author is in agreement with the Gospel of John. Yes, Jesus did prefer Mary to Peter and the others. And in this document Levi takes Mary's part. 'But if the Saviour made her worthy, who are you indeed to reject her? Surely the Saviour knows her very well. That is why he loved her more than us.'[7] In this ancient tradition Jesus knew Mary very well, and loved her more than all women, indeed loved her more than he loved anyone else.

(*c*) *Touching grace*

This kind of tradition was soon pushed to the periphery of the life of the church, as it became dominated by male leadership, celibacy and misogyny. If the Fathers (sic!) of the church had no normal relations with women, it became blasphemous to suggest that Jesus could have had any. Nevertheless the evangelists were agreed that Jesus preferred Mary to Peter and the other disciples, and made her the apostle to the apostles. If ecclesiastical authorities later had problems on this account it was because of their attitudes, not the attitude of Jesus.

With regard to the final moment of recognition we have noted the parallel between the experience of the two travellers to Emmaus, and that of Mary Magdalene. There is no missing the element which distinguishes the two narratives. The one instance is intriguing, the other is intimate. 'Mariam', Jesus addressed her by the name which is remembered in the ancient traditions to which we have referred. 'Do not hold me . . . ' A great deal of scholarly literature has been generated by this phrase: much if not most of it seems determined to miss the most obvious point. Let me illustrate. One of the most delightful experiences which a father can have is to return home after a few days of enforced absence, perhaps because of his work. On a summer's evening he might arrive at last at his house, tired out by work and travel. As he walks down the path to the rear of the house he can hear his children playing in the garden. For a few moments he stands and watches them, himself unobserved. But then they catch sight of him and with shrieks of joy rush towards him to clasp him by the legs, to take his hands, to try to clamber into his arms. Such is an experience of pure grace: without prompting or planning their one reaction is to rush forward to hold him. Should the father be carrying some fragile gift for his wife it would be as well to set it down earlier, for there is no stopping the loving stampede, no compromise to caution.

'Do not touch me . . . ' makes sense only if the spontaneous reaction of Mary at the sight of Jesus, at the sound of her name from a voice which she thought had gone forever, was to rush forward and throw her arms around him. Scholars have concentrated on metaphysical reasons for not touching, but have almost entirely to a man (sic!) avoided recognizing that most intimate human situation in which such a prohibition could arise.

In the Good Friday meditation we warned that Jesus must be allowed to enjoy life as well as suffer from it if he was to be human. In part to test the reaction to the suggestion we considered the possibility that he might have been sexually aroused by the action of the woman who wiped his feet with her hair. In another of these ancient sources to which we have just referred the writer warns: 'Fear not the flesh nor love it. If you fear it, it will gain mastery over you. If you love it, it will swallow and paralyze you.'[8] The orthodox theology of the church up to the Reformation was marked by increasingly neurotic attitudes towards sexuality which far from raising humanity to a higher level, indicated the extent to which these writers had in their fear of it fallen under its mastery. In the document from which we have just quoted we have a much more wholesome human picture of the true humanity of Jesus.

> And the companion of the Saviour is Mary Magdalene. But Christ loved her more than all the disciples and used to kiss her often on her mouth. The rest of the disciples were offended by it and expressed disapproval. They said to him, 'Why do you love her more than all of us?' The Saviour answered and said to them, 'Why do I not love you like her?'[9]

Earlier in this document there is an association of ideas involving the grace which comes through proclamation of the word, the mouth which proclaims it, kissing, and the kiss of peace, but clearly the relationship here described between Jesus and Mary is more than a metaphor! There is grace which comes through preaching, but there are other sources of grace. I have not exaggerated in describing as an experience of pure grace the reaching out and touching of children. Even if at times we disguise it from ourselves we can see in the behaviour of other mammals the fundamental need we humans have for gracious touching and holding.

(*d*) *The spiritual woman*

In these ancient sources we find traditions preserved which do not agree with the theology of the church as it developed, but which are coherent with the Gospels themselves. They tell of Mary Magdalene, and of the true humanity of Jesus. But this alternative tradition about Mary Magdalene did not die out. It reemerged in the mediaeval period. Indeed it is instructive to see how precisely when celibate male theology displayed its most neurotic phobias about women, there was in mediaeval Europe a much more wholesome picture of the truly religious woman, the woman of profound spiritual insight, Mary Magdalene.

In the dominant tradition she was demonized quite falsely as the great sinner, and became the symbol of hope and forgiveness to all who had fallen. But in the mediaeval period, both in France and Germany she was pictured once again as an apostle: she preached and baptized and had the authority to consecrate bishops. As

Elisabeth Moltmann-Wendel says, 'her charismatic personality, forgotten for centuries, like Sleeping Beauty, was awakened'.[10] In the dominant tradition her beauty was her burden, her sensuousness the source of her despair. In contrast this mediaeval picture rejoiced in such beauty and celebrated it with great energy and joy. She was no longer a symbol of the inferiorization of woman, no longer the mirror in which was reflected the neuroses of celibate men. This Mary Magdalene was the patroness of the mediaeval cosmetic industry.

> Artists painted her in elegant flowing dresses decorated with jewellery. In some pictures of the sixteenth and seventeenth-centuries she stands half-nude in front of a mirror, admiring her own beauty. Along with the judgment that this is empty vanity, one senses, even in a prudish Christianity, the pleasure and zest that depict the fun side of life. The beautiful Helen of Christianity skips along at the side of her lover: she rides in the hunt and becomes, when emancipated from the church, a picture of purest delight to the senses.[11]

Nothing renders the Gospels so alien, the Christian landscape so barren as the absence of such delight to the senses. The reason is not difficult to discern, though we are conditioned to deny it. Let me illustrate from an apparently unlikely source.

In June 1843 Karl Marx was at last able to marry his fiancée, Jenny von Westphalen, after many years of postponement. Their first child was born, appropriately on May Day, 1844. In his writings of that time Marx was considering the criteria by which it would be possible to say that a society was becoming more human and humane. In contrast to many today, many who consider themselves Christian, he did not select any economic or material indicators of progress or growth. He began at a very different point:

> the relation of man to woman is the most natural relation of human being to human being. It therefore reveals the extent to which man's natural behaviour has become human, or the extent to which the human essence in him has become a natural essence – the extent to which his human essence has come to be natural to him.[12]

As a species mankind has a natural life, involving biological relations between men and women. Marx contrasts the animal, the biological, the natural, with the specifically human. The specifically human does not arise from the despising or rejecting of the biological, but its transcendence. The same actions take place, but they now express not biological necessity, but a higher form of life, the specifically human yes, the spiritual. The spiritual life, and for Christians this is the life lived by the Spirit of Christ, is not the rejection of sensuousness, but its gracious fulfilment.

The Gospel accounts of Easter do not begin with the male disciples. Instead, the evangelists are agreed that Mary Magdalene was designated by Jesus himself, apostle to the apostles. Mariam was preferred to Simon Peter. She is the model of faith, the exemplar of the spiritual life. And how are we to understand the truly spiritual life? On several occasions we have reflected on the humanity of Jesus. If he was more human than we, not less, then he must have experienced the range of gracious, loving relationships which characterize the truly human life. We have just been considering the picture of Mary Magdalene in mediaeval spirituality. Luther, a man more of that mediaeval world than the modern, claimed of Mary Magdalene's relationship to Jesus: she 'loved him with a hearty, lusting, rutting love'.[13] Are you offended by that thought? I should be delighted for Jesus and for his Mariam if it were true.

11

Resurrection

(*a*) *Putting the question*

There are many things to be discussed at this time, but so far as most Christians are concerned we shall not have dealt with Easter till we have addressed ourselves to the question of the resurrection. Christ is risen: Christ is risen indeed. Yet no one in the early church ever claimed to have observed the resurrection. Instead we have accounts of the appearances of Jesus to the disciples and followers after his death, and the empowerment of Pentecost. We can see the parallel with the subject of the empty tomb. Before we can get started in the Christian faith this question is raised. Did the resurrection happen? Could it have happened? And once again we are faced with the same dilemma. If the resurrection was a historical event, the question whether it happened or not can only admit of a historical answer. Faith cannot guarantee the occurrence of historical events. It would be nice if it could, and certainly it would avoid a great deal of hard work sifting through sources. But if it is claimed that the resurrection was a historical event, then whether we should accept that it happened or not must depend solely on the available data. There is therefore a parallel between the discussion of the empty tomb and of the resurrection, except that there is the further difficulty already noted: no one ever claimed to have observed the resurrection.

This means that the resurrection comes to us not as an event, but as a conclusion drawn from other events. It is not presented to us as the observation of the early church, but rather as the church's interpretation of other events which were experienced, namely the appearance and the empowerment. Not for the first time therefore we must conclude that we are being asked the wrong question. Questions are dangerous forms of speech. They raise doubts in our minds about things we have taken for granted. But they also predispose us to respond within particular parameters. Some questions corral us into answers which misrepresent the situation. 'Have you stopped beating your wife?' Other questions confuse us by taking our language too literally. 'Where does the fire go when it goes out?' There are such dangers too in the apparently straightforward question. 'Did the resurrection happen or not?' It assumes that we know what resurrection is. All we have to do is determine whether it took place or not. A moment's reflection makes it clear that we have but the vaguest idea as to what resurrection might mean. As we shall discover soon, even Paul was far from clear about it. 'Did it happen?' We neither know what the 'it' might be, nor do we know what would count as it 'happening'. We should therefore approach the subject by another route. In the first place we should ask about the events which those at that time did claim to have observed and experienced. This we have already done, in dealing with the appearances and the empowerment. It should be noted that we described these events without speaking about resurrection. But secondly we should ask what resurrection meant to those who first used the term in the early church. And thirdly, to tie the two together, we should ask not whether the resurrection happened, but whether and to what extent the term resurrection is an appropriate way of describing what we know to have happened.

If questions can corral us into alternatives which misrepresent the situation, so can the terms we use. Science proceeds by classification. If a new element or species is discovered it will be best understood when it is seen not as itself, but as a novel form of something already known. We are inclined to do this also with people. What does he do? Where does she shop? If we can typify the person then we assume we shall know him or her. In each case we impose catagories from the known to enable us to understand the unknown. The same procedure is employed in describing events. Although history never repeats itself we use existing terminology to characterize events as they happen. Since our understanding comes from the past we fit the present into its Procrustean bed. We can ask 'Did the crusades happen?' Or we can ask, 'Did the greed, ambition, carnage and mayhem of the mediaeval invasions of the Middle East deserve to be called crusades?' I hope the point of all this will be clear. We are not going to ask 'Did the resurrection happen?' Rather we are going to enquire about the meaning of the term resurrection, and then the appropriateness of its use in describing the objective events from which Christian faith arose.

(*b*) *Sectarian expectations*

The first Christians, like Jesus himself, were Jews and the Hebrew scriptures were to them the word of God. We expect sacred texts to be uniformly edifying, but in a favourite passages of the Bible competition I cannot see Genesis chapter 36 showing well. It begins with a list of the descendents of Esau born in Canaan, followed by a list of those born in Seir. Then there is a list of the sons, at least the chief sons of Esau. Thereafter we have the sons of Seir the Horite. Then we are introduced to the sons of Shobal. The chapter draws to a close with a list of the kings of Edom, and ends with the names of the chiefs of Esau. Clearly the religion of Israel was the religion of a people who were well aware from whence they came. But it was also a religion which knew where it was going. The prophets were remarkable men who could foretell the future. They were specific in the predictions of the downfall of kings and nations. They did not shelter behind ambiguity in the manner of the Greek oracles. They were inspired men who spoke with divine authority. They were sensitive to the future consequences of contemporary events.

However, as we approach the first century of the Christian era this prophetic voice had given way to a more extreme form of prediction. In contrast to prophesies which extrapolated from the mundane, these predictions dealt with the very end of history and therefore went beyond all possible experience. Orthodoxy tends to regard extremism with distaste and disdain. This populist form of religion is referred to as Sectarian Judaism in contrast to the orthodoxy of the schools, the Pharisees and Sadduccees. It was to this Sectarian form that the disciples and followers of Jesus belonged, for the most part. One of the central concerns of this movement was resurrection. Our first question therefore is not whether the resurrection happened, but what did resurrection mean for these Sectarian Jews? Our second question is how appropriate was the term resurrection in describing the objective events? Something happened and they called it resurrection. There was clearly a great advantage to them in doing this. They could use a category which they understood and which would be understood by those Sectarian Jews to whom they preached. But was there a cost as well as a benefit? Was there a Procrustean aspect? Was the uniqueness of the event forced into conformity with existing expectations and beliefs? This is an important and complex issue. You would not expect anything else in dealing with the resurrection. In order to clarify what happened it would be as well to offer two parallel examples of the church's application of terms borrowed from Sectarian Judaism.[1]

The first is Messiah (Greek: *Christos*). The title already had a fairly clear meaning for Sectarian Jews when it was applied to Jesus. The parallel to our discussion of the resurrection is therefore to ask, 'Did the Messiah come or not?' The title Messiah had a long history. Originally, as its etymology suggests, it referred to the anointed one. God chooses a particular person for a special task. It came to refer more narrowly to the king as God's anointed. Especially in time of trouble the people longed for a king like David who would come to deliver them.

Lord, where is thy steadfast love of old,
which by thy faithfulness thou didst swear to David? (Ps. 89.49).

But as empire succeeded empire it became clear that a human king, even of the house of David, would not be sufficient. In the first century of the Christian era the more extreme, apocalyptic movement to which we have referred looked to a supernatural agent of God who would come to deliver his people: 'this is the Messiah whom the Most High has kept until the end of days, who will arise from the posterity of David, and will come and speak to them . . . ' (II Esdras 12.32). Messiah was therefore the title of an expected supernatural agent who would suddenly appear on earth, to initiate a time of tribulation and strife the like of which had never been seen. He would defeat the forces both of the empire and of evil and establish the Kingdom of God, in which the Jews would have a special place. Whenever conditions deteriorated the cry would reach to heaven for God to send his Messiah. At certain festivals expectations would rise. For example the Feast of Dedication, modelled on the ancient Feast of Tabernacles, commemorated the victory of Judas Maccabeus in 165 BC and a brief period of independence for the Jews. At that festival the people wondered whether God would now send his Messiah.

We have taken some time over this matter because it provides an instructive parallel which will help us to deal with the resurrection. There could hardly have been a greater contrast between the Messiah and Jesus. The one a supernatural figure who would suddenly appear full grown, the other born in Nazareth of all places whose family was well enough known. The one figure was anointed specifically to wield weapons and destroy his enemies, the other anointed to suffer at the hands of those who feared and hated him. The one who would not rest till both empire and evil had been destroyed, the other who would be defeated by both. Such was the measure of the contrast between the two. When one came it would mark the beginning of the end of the kingdoms of this world; his coming would bring the history of the world to its conclusion. It must be said of the other that his coming was almost entirely unnoticed outside the immediate sphere of his family and friends: the course of world history continued for the most part unaware, unaffected and indifferent to his fate. When we ask the straight-forward question, 'Did the Messiah come, or not?' the answer is clearly, 'No he did not.'

But the Messiah was only speculation, only a title, a rather exotic way of speaking about God and how God's will would certainly be done. The coming of the Messiah was speculation, the coming of Jesus was fact. The role and character of the Messiah were determined by how people at that time understood God and his dealings with men and women. But what if there was a new revelation of God, a new discernment of the ways of God? The Militant Messiah would certainly not come, nor legions of angels. Instead we should say that the Messiah, the anointed, would look very different both in role and character. His mission and accomplishments would be very different indeed. We should not ask whether the Messiah, already known, has come. Rather we should ask about Jesus, and how the title Messiah must be changed in the light of what was achieved and revealed. History corrects speculation. The revelation is *in* the events.

A second term which the early church took from Sectarian Judaism and applied to Jesus was the title Son of Man. As used for example in Ezekiel, it was originally a colloquial designation rather than a title. It began to develop towards becoming a title in the book of Daniel, a book which is an early example of the apocalyptic movement to which we have been referring. There it appears in a vision of the judgment day at the end of history.

> and behold with the clouds of heaven
> there came one like a son of man,
> and he came to the Ancient of Days
> and was presented before him.
> And to him was given dominion
> and glory and kingdom . . . (Dan. 7.13–14).

The picture of the Son of Man was further developed in the literature of the apocalyptic movement in the first century of the Christian era. He was a sovereign, future figure, whose coming would bring judgment and suffering on earth. In contrast to the Militant Messiah the Son of Man would be a righteous figure, who would redeem the world.

We shall not spend any more time on this figure except to say that there is a similar contrast between the supernatural apocalyptic Son of Man and Jesus of Nazareth. The coming of the Son of Man would cause suffering, but he himself would not suffer. By his judgment he would redeem, but it would not be by his blood that redemption would come. We can therefore briefly go through the same sequence as before. 'Did the Son of Man come or not?' Clearly he did not. The world did not come to an end. But if there was a new revelation of how God deals with people, including those who set themselves against him, then of course this agent would not come. The Son of Man was not historical; the life of Jesus was. And through what was revealed in his suffering and death God's way of redeeming his people was transformed. We should not ask whether the Son of Man came or not, but how must that title be transformed for it to be useful in describing what was achieved and revealed in Jesus. History corrects speculation. The revelation is *in* the events.

We turn now to a third example of a term which the early church took over from Sectarian Judaism. If we are restrained and careful enough then we can follow the same sequence as with the other two examples, Messiah and Son of Man. But can we be sufficiently disciplined to do this? Shall we not continually be tempted to fall back into the old question, 'Did the resurrection happen or not?' If we can be sufficiently restrained then we shall make the breakthrough.

(*c*) *Keeping faith*

Resurrection was another term used by the apocalyptic movement, this popular amorphous grouping which took up ancient truths and pressed them in an increasingly extreme direction. My first book was the work of my youth, and on reading it Philip Larkin observed that it did not deal with death. He chided me that religion should deal with the great issues of life, including death. I am not convinced that every book about religion must deal with death, but he was quite correct about religion in the broad sweep. Christianity has been much concerned, at times obsessively concerned, with death, but the Old Testament says surprisingly little about the subject. It shared with many other cultures the view that the spirits of the dead inhabit an underworld, languid and uninviting. But to this common structure was added a moral dimension: God the judge of men and nations consigned some people to hell. Ezekiel delivered the judgment upon the Egypt of the pharaohs:

> I will make the nations quake at the sound of its fall, when I cast it down to Sheol with those who go down to the Pit . . . (Ezek. 31.16).

Alternatively, the righteous judge can redeem from hell.

For great is thy steadfast love toward me;
thou has delivered my soul from the depths of Sheol (Ps. 86.13).

A strong theme running through the Old Testament is that of covenant. It distinguished the religion of ancient Israel, and Judaism, from all other religions of the ancient world. God has made an agreement with his people. If they obey the terms of the covenant, he will be their God. We have already referred to the procession of empires which arose and dominated the Jews. Frequently the prophets interpreted the defeat of the nation as God's way of punishing their unfaithfulness to the covenant. But how were they to interpret that very different situation in which righteous Jews suffered persecution and even death in order to keep the covenant? The book of Daniel, to which we have already referred, was written in a time of persecution, when the Seleucid king Antiochus Epiphanes cruelly murdered those who would not give up their religion or at least compromise its demands. This led to the question, will God keep faith with those who keep faith with him? And if so, how will he keep faith with those who go down to death before his Kingdom is established? There could be but one answer: God will raise them up on that day. Resurrection therefore was the speculative term they used to describe this rising again from death to life.

Can we be sufficiently restrained to follow the sequence? 'Did resurrection happen?' The answer is No. The Messiah did not come as predicted, not the Militant Messiah. The Son of Man did not come as expected, the one who shed other people's blood, but not his own. And now we must say, resurrection did not occur in the terms expected. It would happen when history was brought to an end, when the judgment took place, when the righteous who had been faithful unto death were vindicated and raised to new life. By contrast the world did not come to an end with the death of Jesus nor did the dead rise to new life. The great and terrible Day of the Lord did not materialize. The general resurrection predicted for that time did not happen. Resurrection did not happen; but the life of Jesus did. We should not ask 'Did resurrection happen or not?', because that speculation arose from a previous understanding of how God deals with the world. If a new revelation has been discerned then we should rather ask whether and to what extent the old term resurrection can usefully be employed to describe what did happen.

And what did happen? This is the most dangerous point of all. We are in danger of setting aside everything which has been said, and reverting to the story of the empty tomb. Can we resist this and follow our sequence? What happened? Two things, already discussed. The appearances of Jesus after his death, and the empowerment of his disciples and followers. The question is not whether the resurrection happened, but whether this new revelation can be usefully described by that term, and if not how it must be freshly interpreted. History corrects speculation. The mystery is *in* the events. But the events are the appearances and the empowerment, not the empty tomb and resurrection.

We are normally expected to begin with the empty tomb and proceed towards Pentecost. In fact we should move in the opposite direction. Pentecost is not an appendage to the empty tomb: the empty tomb is a conclusion drawn from Pentecost. Pentecost is not an entailment of the resurrection; resurrection is the interpretation which the early Christians (Sectarian Jews) gave to their experience.

No one in the early church ever claimed to have observed the resurrection, but since resurrection was a term which was available to them, like Messiah or Son of Man, they applied it to describe their experience of the appearances and the empowerment. The resurrection was not an event, but the interpretation of other events. Those of us who are not Sectarian Jews may well find that the term resurrection is more problematic than helpful. The empty tomb was not an event, but a deduction from the belief that resurrection had taken place. If we do not believe that the Militant Messiah came; if we do not believe that the non-suffering Son of Man came, neither do we believe that the resurrection, the rising at the end of the world, occurred. The old beliefs in Messiah, Son of Man and resurrection, beliefs which arose from previous beliefs about God, were all discredited at Pentecost. We know what happened at Pentecost and it is the basis of our faith. That is what we must defend, and can defend. Whether we can use the old terms to describe the new revelation is another matter. To continue to use the term Messiah requires a fundamental and complete reinterpretation of it. Whether we can continue to use the term Son of Man in the light of the new revelation depends on giving it a completely new meaning. Can we be restrained enough to say the same about resurrection? Whether we continue to use this term, a term which arose from old and now overtaken beliefs about God, will depend on whether it can be completely changed to usefully and adequately describe what happened to Jesus.

(*d*) *No turning back*

If we still use the title Messiah, it is because there has been a reversal. It had a clear meaning among Sectarians, expressing their understanding of God. If we believed that this Militant Messiah had come, then we should be Sectarian Jews. But we do not believe such a figure appeared, and we are not Sectarian Jews. That is the reversal. We do not use the term with its clear meaning to tell us about Jesus. To the contrary, we allow what happened in Jesus, this new revelation of the invisible God, to redefine the meaning of Messiah. He is the agent of God by whom God has overcome the power of evil and through whom his Kingdom will come. The mystery is *in* the events, and that new disclosure gives a radically new meaning to the title Messiah.

Through the wonders of computing I am now going to instruct

my word processor to repeat the previous paragraph verbatim, changing only the title discussed and one or two associated terms from Messiah to Son of Man. If we still use the title Son of Man, it is because there has been a reversal. It had a clear meaning among Sectarians, expressing their understanding of God. If we believed that this aloof Redeemer had come, then we should be Sectarian Jews. But we do not believe such a figure appeared, and we are not Sectarian Jews. That is the reversal. We do not use the term with its clear meaning to tell us about Jesus. To the contrary, we allow what happened in Jesus, this new revelation of the invisible God, to redefine the meaning of Son of Man. He is the agent of God by whom God has redeemed the world through the shedding of his own blood. The mystery is *in* the events, and that new disclosure gives a radically new meaning to the title Son of Man.

Finally, I shall repeat the same paragraph verbatim again, applying it now to our immediate subject. If we still use the term resurrection, it is because there has been a reversal. It had a clear meaning among Sectarians, expressing their understanding of God. If we believed that this event of resurrection had taken place, then we should be Sectarian Jews. But we do not believe such an event has taken place, and we are not Sectarian Jews. That is the reversal. We do not use the term with its clear meaning to tell us about Jesus. To the contrary, we allow what happened in Jesus, this new revelation of the invisible God, to redefine the meaning of resurrection. He is the agent of God by whom God has overcome the power of death and the alienation of hell. The mystery is *in* the events, and that new disclosure gives a radically new meaning to the term resurrection.

Although the term resurrection could be readily applied by those early Christians who had been Sectarian Jews, it is not without danger. Oh the high drama of it all! Angels form a guard of honour at the tomb. At the first hour on the first day there is a blast of heavenly trumpets that not even the walls of Jericho could have resisted, and the great stone first trembles and then is tossed aside like a pebble. It is rolled back, symbolic of the events of the last few days. Death is rolled back. History is rolled back. Jesus walks again with his disciples and followers, breaking bread, eating some broiled fish. That is the faith of the empty tomb and the resurrection, but it is not our faith. Why? Because the mystery is *in* the events and the greatest danger is to think that the events can be rolled back. That way the mystery itself is eliminated, and instead of a new revelation of God we have the old God negating history, nullifying the very events in which the new was disclosed.

If resurrection is still to be used, it must now be used not according to the old faith of Sectarian Judaism, but to express the experience of the new faith of Christians. It has nothing to do with an empty tomb and a body getting up and walking about again. It has everything to do with the new life of the Spirit which came at Pentecost. Not *mana*, not *wakanda*, but the Spirit of Jesus Christ of Nazareth. This is the real victory over death, the true disclosure of the deep things of life, the final revelation of God *in* the one who was crucified.

12

Those Who Have Not Seen

(*a*) *New faith for old*

There are many examples throughout church history of situations in which the authorities, the guardians of orthodoxy, have held a rather dismissive view of popular religion. We have already noted that this was true of the attitude of the Sadduccees and Pharisees towards Sectarian Judaism. But on at least one issue the Pharisees were in agreement with populist beliefs, in contrast to the Sadduccees. Although it was not strictly speaking a scriptural doctrine, they too believed in the resurrection of the dead. It was a considerable theological and social step for Saul the Pharisee to take when he became Paul the apostle of Jesus Christ, but at least on this one issue he did not have to leave his former beliefs behind: with Sectarian Judaism and the Christian church he believed in the resurrection of the dead. Indeed this was the problem.

Paul was not converted to a completely new religion. In the first place at the time of his conversion there was no Christian religion. He is remembered as one who was converted to Christianity in the earliest days of the church and consequently as one of those responsible for the development of its life and doctrine. But in writing to the Galatians Paul claims that on his conversion he immediately went off to Arabia and then Damascus for three years, having no contact with the churches in Judaea. Even after that he spent just two weeks in Jerusalem and saw only Peter and James, before going off again to Syria for fourteen years. There was no new religion to which he could be converted, but clearly he did not simply adhere to the new faith as it was evolving and developing in Jerusalem and Judaea.

The earliest Christians were all Jews, and nearly all belonged within that broad populist movement now referred to as Sectarian Judaism. It never occurred to them that they were initiating a new religion. Nor were they, at that point. The events surrounding the ministry of Jesus, his death and their experiences immediately thereafter were all understood within their own existing religious tradition. For this reason they interpreted them in the terms available to them, including Messiah, Son of Man – and resurrection. As we have seen this was a mixed blessing. The terms helped them to understand what had happened, but only if these same terms were substantially reinterpreted. What would be a sufficient reinterpretation for them, would later prove insufficient for new converts who did not come from their religious background.

When Paul was converted there was therefore no new religion. There was the beginning of a new sect within Judaism, those known as the followers of the Way. He was converted as he travelled to Damascus. Why did he not return to Jerusalem and associate with the church there and its leaders? Two reasons suggest themselves, one practical, the other theological. The practical one, the more obvious but in the long term the less important, was that he had until that moment been identified as a persecutor of the church. He was a man of great moral courage and integrity, but it may be that just then he could not face the families of those whom he had caused to be arrested. And in view of his own zeal it would be likely if ironic that he in turn would have been arrested should he have suddenly reappeared in the city to proclaim those things for which he had persecuted others. The more theological reason is that even at that stage his understanding of the new faith was different from that of the leaders of the church. They found in it the fulfilment of Sectarian Judaism. He found in it the fulfilment of Pharisaic Judaism. They brought with them their previous religious terms and concerns, to find them reinterpreted but nevertheless in that sense confirmed. He did not begin with their religious terms or concerns and therefore was not converted to their new faith. If Paul was the first Pharisee to be converted then it was for him to discover how the new faith was the fulfilment of his old faith. In this the leaders of the church in Jerusalem could be of little help. We can understand that he would wish to go off for some time prayerfully to reflect on these things. Three years is longer than might be expected, but if he then spent only two weeks with the leaders in Jerusalem it would seem that his understanding of the new faith was fundamentally different from theirs. To go off then for fourteen years indicates not only how fundamental the differences were but how difficult it was to conceive of the new Christian faith as the fulfilment of the faith by which he had previously lived.

Paul never ceased to be a Jew of the Pharisaic tradition, but when at last he did return to Jerusalem he was convinced that the old faith was fulfilled in the new, that in Christ were the answers to the problems which had faced him in Pharisaic Judaism. It therefore seems more than a little ironic that it was at this point that he was appointed apostle to the Gentiles! They had never been Pharisees and did not accept the premises of the old faith. It was therefore inevitable that Paul would soon find himself alienated even from those who responded to his preaching. They could not accept the things which he had brought into Christianity from his previous religious tradition. Thus he was critical of their Gentile, Hellenistic views of the relationship between Christians and the state. He was appalled by their social life, including as it did participation in local festivals which retained aspects of civil religion. He was affronted by the liberal and liberated place of women within the churches. And of special interest to us in this context, he was dismayed at their attitude towards resurrection.

(*b*) *Vain faith*

What was the faith of the church in Corinth? More fundamental than their beliefs was the empowerment of the Spirit of Jesus Christ of Nazareth. We have already discussed the gifts of the Spirit with which they were blessed, including that contentious gift of speaking in tongues. But if we turn to their beliefs then the Good News would bring them the true knowledge of God, the knowledge of the true God. It would reverse their understanding of themselves, and the society in which they lived. That is to say they would now believe what previously would have seemed folly to them as Gentiles. And above all, in that Hellenistic culture, the new faith would bestow meaning upon their lives, a meaning which was not threatened by that last enemy, death.

Just as the new faith addressed those things most important to Paul, it addressed those concerns most central to the Gentiles of Corinth. And the two were not the same. If we use our three examples again then we can say firstly that they would not be concerned about the coming of a Messiah of the house of David. But they experienced God's power on earth through Jesus. Indeed the word 'Christ' soon lost its meaning as an eschatological title and became almost a proper name: Jesus Christ of Nazareth. Secondly they would not be concerned with the apocalyptic figure of the Son of Man. Indeed the title quickly disappeared from the Gentile churches. It had been the richest title available to the Sectarians, more subtle than Messiah, but it was so closely related to that very complex movement that it was more trouble than it was worth to explain it to the Gentiles. Gentile Christians therefore ceased to use the title, but of course they were concerned with the same issue. They experienced God as Redeemer in the life and death of Jesus. And thirdly, it would seem that they were not much interested in the term resurrection, so much connected with that rich mixture of patriotism and religion characteristic of the Maccabean period. But they were concerned that they had received eternal life now in the Spirit of Jesus.

The Gentile church in Corinth experienced the reality of Christian faith, but the terms in which they appropriated it were inevitably different from those which were important to Paul. After all, the terms in which he had appropriated it were different from those of the Jerusalem church. There was therefore always the danger that Paul would think that when they rejected the terms, they rejected the reality. If they were indifferent to the terms which made sense to him, they would appear to be indifferent to the substance of the faith itself. Clearly this was not so, but it may well be the basis of his warning to them in I Corinthians 15 about rejecting the resurrection.

> But if there is no resurrection of the dead, then Christ has not been raised; if Christ has not been raised, then our preaching is in vain and your faith is in vain.

Earlier we distinguished between what happened, the appearances and the empowerment, and the interpretation of the event, namely resurrection. The Corinthian church certainly did not lack the empirical evidence of the Spirit: Paul tells us as much. But apparently they did not interpret that empowerment as being confirmation of the speculation, both Sectarian and Pharisaic, concerning resurrection. Hence the disagreement. They recognized the event, empowerment, but not the interpretation, resurrection. Paul believed that his previous faith in resurrection had been confirmed by the empowerment. For him to reject the resurrection was to set aside the whole basis of the faith. That might have been true for him: clearly it was not so for them.

> If Christ has not been raised, your faith is futile and you are still in your sins. Then those also who have fallen asleep in Christ have perished. If for this life only we have hoped in Christ, we are of all men most to be pitied.

Given Paul's former views on law, sin and righteousness, the forgiveness of sins takes place only on the basis of the resurrection. However, the Corinthians had experienced the Spirit of forgiveness and reconciliation. Nor was their hope for this life only. They experienced eternal life now, and it was on this that their hope was based. The basis of their faith was the empowerment of the Spirit: resurrection was an interpretation which added nothing for them. Paul assumed that to be indifferent to resurrection was to undermine both faith and hope. His new faith was still based on premises which came from his old faith. This is demonstrated in the next phase of his argument.

> But in fact Christ has been raised from the dead, the first fruits of those who have fallen asleep. For as by a man came death, by a man has come also the resurrection of the dead. For as in Adam all die, so also in Christ shall all be made alive. But each in his own order: Christ the first fruits, then at his coming those who belong to Christ.

As we have already noted, the problem with interpreting the appearances and the empowerment as resurrection is that resurrection as expected did not take place. The resurrection would come at the end of the age, a general resurrection of the faithful who had died before the judgment day. Since this did not happen the resurrection of Jesus had to be radically reinterpreted. He is now the first fruits, the first instalment. That is not what resurrection meant, and in any case the end of history did not come about. The judgment day did not materialize. Small wonder that the Gentile Christians did not find this way of speaking about their experience appropriate. To them it made more sense to say that the life of the Spirit is that foretaste of eternal life with Christ. They also believed 'that the last enemy to be destroyed is death'. Of that they were sure: of the speculative concept of resurrection they were unsure.

But Paul identified the two. If they did not use the term

resurrection then they had no faith that death had been overcome, no hope for life eternal. 'If the dead are not raised, "Let us eat and drink, for tomorrow we die." ' For Paul those who do not affirm the resurrection affirm nothing, and might as well adopt a completely libertine life-style, for there is nothing but this life. In passing we might note that this is a slur on those atheists and agnostics who commit themselves to high moral standards, often at great personal cost, because even if this life is all there is that is how they want to live this life. To live the moral life only because of the possible reward of a life to come would generally be regarded as itself immoral. But in any case that was not the position of the Corinthians. They may not all and always have adhered to the moral standards advocated by Paul, but they believed in life after death: they experienced it here and now, or the first fruits of it.

We have indicated that the speculative concept of resurrection had to be fundamentally reinterpreted to be appropriated by non-Jewish Christian communities such as that in Corinth. A single resurrection had not been envisaged, and certainly not one separated from the Day of the Lord. But there is another problem which arises from using the term resurrection. It surely implies a material rising, a somatic, embodied rising from the dead. Otherwise there is no problem at all: we can speak of spirits appearing. That way lies Docetism, but in any case it would be the negation of Judaism, both Sectarian and Pharisaic. By insisting that what has happened must be called resurrection Paul set himself an insuperable problem, one which indeed calls into question the usefulness of this whole approach.

(*c*) *A spiritual body*

It was bad enough that at least some of the Corinthians decided that they could not make sense of the idea of resurrection, but worse was to come when Paul attempted to explain it to them.

> But some one will ask, 'How are the dead raised? With what kind of body do they come?' You foolish man! What you sow does not come to life unless it dies. And what you sow is not the body which is to be, but a bare kernel, perhaps of wheat or of some other grain.

I wonder if any one in Corinth followed that argument. Paul was given to a mosaic style of arguing: one image suggested another.

Yes, a seed must die: Jesus used that metaphor of nature to illustrate a spiritual truth. But when the seed of an oak tree dies, it is another oak tree which springs up. It is not at all clear what light all this throws upon the question of a resurrection body. But Paul berated his questioners because he was being asked a question he could not answer satisfactorily. The more he blusters, the more suspicious we become. At the outset it seemed that the Corinthians had a problem. But as the matter proceeds we begin to glimpse a rather different problem. The Corinthians did not need an answer to the question. It was not their problem. But having offered to provide an answer Paul becomes enmeshed in an ever more convoluted line of argument. It would seem that an answer must be given, not for their sake, but for his.

> But God gives a body as he has chosen, and to each kind of seed its own body. For not all flesh is alike, but there is one kind for men, another for animals, another for birds, and another for fish. There are celestial bodies and there are terrestrial bodies; but the glory of the celestial is one, and the glory of the terrestrial is another. There is one glory of the sun, and another glory of the moon, and another glory of the stars; for star differs from star in glory.

On the basis of this one passage alone I should judge that a theory of verbal inspiration of scripture fails. Any probationer being assigned this as the text from which to preach his trial sermon would have good grounds for an appeal. It is not an argument. Am I alone in finding it embarrassing? There are a lot of blustering words designed to silence the Corinthians, but they do not amount to an argument. What kind of body? It would never have occurred to the Corinthians to ask such a question. It arises from Paul's premises, not theirs. But if the question were asked, then the answer is clear: We just do not know. But Paul, in full flight, will not make this simple and humble admission, since he imagines that the whole basis of Christian faith is at stake.

> So it is with the resurrection of the dead. What is sown is perishable, what is raised is imperishable. It is sown in dishonour, it is raised in glory. It is sown in weakness, it is raised in power. It is sown a physical body, it is raised a spiritual body.

There are some interesting assumptions in this passage, not least that our present bodies are 'sown in dishonour'. Really? There is a good deal in the same letter to the Corinthians to suggest misogyny and this seems to arise from the same source. But in any case the Corinthians believed in all of these distinctions without using the term resurrection. Paul made resurrection fundamental to Christian faith, and yet his tortured arguments in trying to cope with the most obvious consequence of this concept surely raise questions about its validity.

Once you insist on interpreting the appearances and the empowerment by use of the speculative concept of resurrection, then you are committed to a material body – of some kind. It is a purely speculative idea. We have no experience of such a thing, and yet it becomes somehow the fundamental tenet of Christian faith, more fundamental than the things we do know about.

There is a corollary, and it is truly alarming. What if we were to decline to use this speculative concept, because we are not intrigued by speculation; what if we deemed that the speculative concept of resurrection is too problematic; what if we were to discover that far from illuminating our faith it distorted it; what if consequently we decided to stay with the things we actually know about, to trust those things which we have experienced; what if in order to be true to our faith we gave up this terminology which derives from assumptions completely foreign to us? What if we were to do this for the sake of faith? We should be told that we had no faith. What an extraordinary reversal. What we know, the deep things of our experience, can be set aside in favour of what we do not know, a speculative belief which has never been confirmed in anyone's experience. In the course of our examination of this subject the concept of resurrection has become increasingly problematic. It leads to further and more serious difficulties, it risks discrediting the faith by attaching to it as necessary elements appendages which are quite extraneous and arbitrary. But there is more and it is worse: there is one further step to which resurrection commits those who use it. A material body, an empty tomb, and finally bodily ascension.

(*d*) *Ascended into heaven*

Whenever I visit the Burrell Collection in Glasgow's Pollok Estate I make a point of going to the display of mediaeval stained glass windows. One in particular never fails to fascinate me. It is neither ornate nor complex. A small group of figures stands in a circle. In the centre there are two footprints, side by side, clearly marked in the fine sand. The figures are looking upwards. The visitor on arriving in front of this scene has the impression that he has just arrived in time, because at the top of the window a pair of feet are just about to disappear. The subject is the ascension, and had he arrived a few seconds later the visitor would have missed Jesus going up to heaven. It is a crude representation, but it is exactly what is required by an insistence on resurrection.

We have insisted that the mystery is *in* the events, but what were the events? So far as the Easter side of the story is concerned the answer must be the appearances and the empowerment. The resurrection was not an event, but the interpretation of other events. The empty tomb was not an event, but the materializing of the appearances, and a deduction from the appearances. When we turn to the ascension we must say that neither was it an event: it was the necessary consequence of the resurrection and the empty tomb. We have already commented on the crude materialism of the view that Jesus rose from the dead in such a form that it was necessary to have the stone rolled away. But this was what was expected of resurrection. Matthew anticipates himself when he describes the moment of Jesus' death.

> And behold, the curtain of the temple was torn in two, from top to bottom; and the earth shook, and the rocks were split; and tombs also were opened, and many bodies of the saints who had fallen asleep were raised, and coming out of the tombs after his resurrection they went into the holy city and appeared to many (Matt. 27.51–3).[1]

It is a convoluted account, since although the dead rise at the moment that Jesus died on the cross, the evangelist has in mind that there is a general resurrection of the (Christian) faithful following the resurrection of Jesus. It is a confusing and anachronistic sequence, but it is quite clear that Matthew maintained the Sectarian view of resurrection. That is to say, it is an eschatological moment at which the resurrection of Jesus is the signal for a general, physical, resurrection of the faithful.

There is in human nature what might be called a more-than-thou attitude. We are all familiar with its holier-than-thou manifestation. But it can take different forms. It can be an attitude of believing-more-than-thou. And the result of this week's *Credal Question Time* is victory by fifteen beliefs to five. Believing things is apparently a virtue. The more incredible the beliefs the more their religious value.[2] A further example of this phenomenon is the more-material-than-thou attitude. On this view nothing is real unless it registers on the Richter scale. Symbol, metaphor, figures of speech: all an atheistic-communist conspiracy. It must be nothing less than earthquake, the veil of the temple ripped from top to bottom, the stone rolled away, the print of the nails, broiled fish. It is a salutary fact that extremes begin to resemble each other. This kind of 'realism' is a form of materialism. As such it is credible as Newton's physics or von Ranke's historicism. Its *reductio ad absurdum* is that since the body is no longer here on earth, it must have gone up to heaven. It would be tasteless to pursue this position to its absurd conclusions: not how did a material body go up, but in modern astronomy what would 'up' mean? Not how did a material body get all the way to heaven, but is heaven also material? Not did the disciples see the body go up, but is it only distance that prevents us from still seeing it? And this is supposed to be more religious, more spiritual, more Christian.

We have already noted that no matter how traditions develop and grow, no matter their later complexities, they very often begin from some historical incident or experience. Again and again we have gone back to the original events, the appearances and the empowerment. There is no doubt, however, that the basis of Christian faith is the empowerment. The appearances by themselves were not enough. This is acknowledged in the opening chapter of Acts.

> 'But you shall receive power when the Holy Spirit has come upon you; and you shall be my witnesses in Jerusalem and in all Judaea and Samaria and to the end of the earth.' And when he had said this, as they were looking on, he was lifted up, and a cloud took him out of their sight. And while they were gazing into heaven as he went, behold, two men stood by them in white robes, and said, 'Men of Galilee, why do you stand looking into heaven? This Jesus, who was taken up from you into heaven, will come in the same way as you saw him go into heaven' (1.8–12).

It is unlikely that the disciples would have come to faith solely through the experience of the Spirit. The appearances prepared them to receive the Spirit as the Spirit of Jesus Christ of Nazareth. The appearances without the Spirit were not enough, but once the connection was made, and the Spirit had come, the appearances were no longer necessary. The faith was based on the experience of his Spirit. Although the appearances were frequent and widespread for the first few weeks, they all but ceased by Pentecost. To have an appearance thereafter was to be born out of season.

Christian faith must be based on those things for which we ourselves can vouch. The faith that God is definitively revealed in Jesus does not depend on an empty tomb. The faith that this revelation, a scandal to religious sensibilities and the contradiction of common sense, does not depend on a bodily resurrection. The faith that the judges were judged and Jesus now stands at the right hand of God does not depend on the ascension. We cannot be expected to affirm such events. Like the man in John's Gospel challenged by the authorities, in the last analysis we can only vouch for what we have experienced: 'one thing I know, that though I was blind, now I see' (9.25). We come too late to be witnesses to historical events, but with great relief we discover that we are no worse off for that: 'Have you believed because you have seen me? Blessed are those who have not seen and yet believe' (20.29).

EPILOGUE

If the mystery is *in* the events, rather than in a theory about them, then the value of these meditations is in the pilgrimage itself, the journeying towards the heart of the matter. There is therefore no place for a Conclusion, however disappointing this may be for those who might want to dispense with reading through the text, making the pilgrimage with us. But there are some things which need to be said about the position we have reached.

Firstly, across the variations of the Gospel accounts of the empty tomb there is a constant theme. 'Why do you seek the living among the dead?' It is natural that we should look to the events from which Christian faith first arose. We have already discussed which were the historical events, and which the later interpretations of these events. It is natural that we should look back to these events, but beginning with Lot's wife we also know that there is an incompatibility between looking back and walking in faith. Faith is not knowledge of events in the past. We have seen that faith cannot fill in the gaps in incomplete historical sources. We can look back to the events from which faith first arose, but knowledge of these events is not a substitute for the grounds of our own faith. In the last analysis the empirical basis of faith is present and not past. It is in the land of the living, not of the dead. It is the empowerment of the Spirit and not an empty tomb.

Secondly, when we speak of empowerment by the Spirit, it is not any spirit: neither *mana*, nor *wakanda* but the Spirit of Jesus Christ of Nazareth. In that name, which is also a title, the past and the present cohere, fact and faith. The one who was now is, the one who was remembered is now experienced. Here is the continuity: the Master is now Lord. He who was defeated is now exalted, he who was condemned is now judge. But this experience of the Spirit also vindicates his teaching and valorizes his practice.

Thirdly, in this coherence of fact and faith the mystery of God is disclosed. As we have seen, the first heresy, the first, most persistent and still present heresy, always tempts us to look to a theory about God to see how Jesus was used by the God already known. To the contrary, we must look to Jesus, to the events of his life and death, to see how God is now disclosed. No Militant Messiah or Servant of Satan, no legions of angels, but rather the God who allows himself to be edged out of the world and on to the cross, the God who calls on us to join him in his suffering at the hands of a godless world.

Fourthly, we are right to attend to the life and teaching, the events of the life and death of Jesus, because they are the parameters within which Christian faith travels and grows. We cannot simply look to the past, as if we could do only what was there commanded, but if the mystery is *in* these events they must act for us as a constraint. There are 'many things' into which we are being led, but negatively nothing can be Christian which is incompatible with what we know of Jesus. Dostoyevsky's Grand Inquisitor was a man who continued to worship the old God, the God of those who rejected Jesus. There are many in the church who resist the Spirit of Jesus Christ out of loyalty to the God already known.

But finally, if we are to seek him among the living and not the dead, as he comes to us from the future and not simply from the past, then he will not always appear as he did then. To those who lived in the Jewish religious world he was the Messiah, the agent of God come with power. To those who lived in the Hellenistic world he was the *Logos*, the reason of all things. To those who lived in the Byzantine world he was *pantocrator*, the unification of a divided world. And what will he be to us today and in the immediate years to come?

> I have yet many things to say to you, but you cannot bear them now. When the Spirit of truth comes, he will guide you into all the truth; for he will not speak on his own authority, but whatever he hears he will speak, and he will declare to you the things that are to come (John 16.12–13).

Neither *mana* nor *wakanda*, the Spirit of Jesus Christ of Nazareth is the spirit of justice, of equity, of reconciliation, of compassion, the basis on which all walls of partition, discrimination and domination are dismantled. This is the world in which we live today. We can be possessed by that Spirit, but we cannot possess or limit it to the concerns of the church. It 'blows where it wills'.

The evidence for the Good News of Easter surrounds us if we have eyes to perceive it.

NOTES

1. The Prisoner of Conscience

1. N. Mandela, *The Struggle is My Life*, International Defence and Aid Fund for Southern Africa, London 1978, p. 175.
2. A. Solzhenitsyn, *The Gulag Archipelago*, Collins 1974, p. 483.
3. Ibid., p. 546.
4. Ibid., p. 130.
5. A. Solzhenitsyn, *The First Circle*, Collins 1970, p. 607.
6. Ibid.

2. The Scandal of the Cross

1. H. Heine, *Memorials of Krahwinkel's Days of Terror*; quoted in S. Korner, *Kant*, Penguin 1955, p. 129.
2. 'The Embassy to Gaium', *Philo's Works*, vol. X, pp. 302f., Loeb Classical Library 1962.
3. Flavius Josephus, 'The Antiquities of the Jews', *Complete Works*, Vol. XVIII.8, Pickering & Inglis 1960.
4. For the incidence of crucifixion in the ancient world see Martin Hengel, *Crucifixion*, SCM Press and Fortress Press 1977; reprinted in *The Cross of the Son of God*, SCM Press 1986.

3. Suffering and Redemption

1. F. Nietzsche, *The Anti-Christ*, Penguin 1968, p. 131.
2. F. Nietzsche, *Thus Spoke Zarathustra*, Penguin 1969, p. 45.
3. P.F. Kirby, quoted in W. Sargant, *Battle for the Mind*, Penguin 1961, p. 116.
4. K. Marx, 'Critique of Hegel's Philosophy of Right: Introduction', in T.B. Bottomore, *Karl Marx: Early Writings*, C.A. Watts & Co. 1963, p. 58.
5. Ibid., p. 43.
6. J. Moltmann, *Theology of Hope*, SCM Press and Harper & Row 1967, p. 21.
7. C. Guevara, *Guerrilla Warfare*, Penguin 1969, p. 15.
8. C. Guevara, *Reminiscences of the Cuban Revolutionary War*, Penguin 1969, p. 183.
9. Ibid., p. 235.
10. F. Castro, 'In Tribute to Che', included in C. Guevara, *Reminiscences of the Cuban Revolutionary War*, p. 26.

4. *Women at the Cross*

1. T. Berakot 7.18

2. This incident does not appear in the best Greek manuscripts, but it is illustrative of the authority with which Jesus took it upon himself to interpret the law.

3. E. Moltmann-Wendel, *Humanity in God*, SCM Press and Pilgrim Press 1983, p. 33.

5. *Death and Dereliction*

1. I. Kurtz, 'Bring Back Death', *The Guardian*, London and Manchester, 13 November 1984.

2. William Shakespeare, *Hamlet*, Act III, Scene i.

6. *We Had Hoped*

1. See H.A. Drake, *In Praise of Constantine*: a historical study and a new translation of Eusebius' Tricennial Orations, University of California Press, Los Angeles 1975, p. 85. See also A. Kee, *Constantine versus Christ*, SCM Press 1982, p. 38.

2. J. Moltmann, *The Crucified God*, SCM Press and Harper & Row 1974, p. 205.

3. D. Bonhoeffer, *Letters and Papers from Prison*, The Enlarged Edition, SCM Press and the Macmillan Company 1971, p. 361.

4. K. Barth, *Church Dogmatics*, T. & T. Clark 1956, I/2, p. 158.

7. *Metamorphosis*

1. The classic presentation of this position, including anthropological material, is G. van der Leeuw, *Religion in Essence and Manifestation*, Peter Smith, Gloucester, Mass. 1967.

2. J. Falwell, *Listen America!*, Bantam Books, New York 1981, p. 12.

3. B. Griffiths, *Monetarism and Morality*: an answer to the bishops, Centre for Policy Studies 1985, p. 8.

4. E. Troeltsch, *The Social Teaching of the Christian Churches*, Harper & Row 1960, vol. 1, p. 63.

5. José Miranda, *Communism in the Bible*, SCM Press and Orbis Books, Maryknoll, 1982, p. 13.

6. Tertullian, *Apology*, Loeb Classical Library 1931.

8. *The Appearances*

1. A. Kee, *The Way of Transendence*, Penguin Books 1972, 2nd edn SCM Press 1985.

9. *The Empty Tomb*

1. R.L. Fox, *Pagans and Christians*, Penguin Books 1988, p. 150.

2. Ibid., p. 141.

3. Offensive though this might at first seem, it is only an intermediate conclusion,

as indicated by John A.T. Robinson: 'For all we can be sure, as Ronald Gregor Smith scandalized many by insisting, the bones of Jesus may still be lying about somewhere in Palestine. And we must be *free* to say so'. *Twelve More New Testament Studies*, SCM Press 1984, pp. 7f.).

10. The Companion of Jesus

1. For patristic references see E. Moltmann-Wendel, *Humanity in God*, SCM Press and Pilgrim Press 1983, p. 11.
2. 'The Dialogue of the Saviour' III.5.139, in J.M. Robinson (ed.), *The Nag Hammadi Library in English*, E.J. Brill 1984.
3. Ibid., 140.
4. C. Schmidt, (ed.), *Pistis Sophia, Nag Hammadi Studies*, Volume IX, E.J. Brill 1978, Book IV, chapter 146.
5. 'The Gospel of Mary' 10, in *The Nag Hammadi Library in English.*
6. Ibid., 17.
7. Ibid., 18.
8. 'The Gospel of Philip' 66, in *The Nag Hammadi Library in English.*
9. Ibid., 63–4.
10. E. Moltmann-Wendel, op. cit., p. 10.
11. Ibid., p. 14.
12. K. Marx, 'The Economic and Philosophical Manuscripts' in K. Marx and F. Engels, *Collected Works*, vol. 3, Lawrence & Wishart 1975, p. 296.
13. *D. Martin Luthers Werke*, Kritische Gesamtausgabe, Weimar 1883–, 28:449, 32,35.

11. Resurrection

1. A useful summary of the meaning of these central themes is given in D.S. Russell, *The Method and Message of Jewish Apocalyptic*, SCM Press and Westminster Press 1964.

12. Those Who Have Not Seen

1. For an interesting note on the attitude of Jews of the period to the bones of their deceased relatives, see J.D.G. Dunn, *The Evidence for Jesus*, SCM Press and Westminster Press 1985, p. 66. For a fascinating account of the Mount of Olives as the location of the death and resurrection of Jesus, see E.L. Martin, *Secrets of Golgotha*, ASK, Alhambra, California 1988. Martin moves like a detective in a mystery story to uncover the historical events of the death of Jesus, beginning with the centurion's words at the cross (Luke 23.47). The torn curtain of the temple could only have been seen from the Mount of Olives.
2. Tertullian, 'On the Flesh of Christ', *Ante-Nicene Christian Library*, vol. 15, *The Writings of Tertullian*, T. & T. Clark 1871, chapter 5, section 22–6.